Your Government Inaction

ROGER BRUNS and
GEORGE VOGT

ST. MARTIN'S PRESS
New York

Copyright © 1981 by Roger Bruns and George Vogt

All rights reserved. For information, write:
St. Martin's Press, Inc., 175 Fifth Ave., New York, N.Y. 10010.

Manufactured in the United States of America

Library of Congress Cataloging in Publication Data

Bruns, Roger.
  Your government inaction.

  1. Administrative agencies—United States—Records
and correspondence. 2. Government correspondence.
3. Memorandums. 4. Public administration—Anecdotes,
facetiae, satire, etc. I. Vogt, George, joint author.
II. Title.
JK468.C75B78   353′.000207   80-24170
ISBN 0-312-89814-2 (pbk.)

Design by Dennis J. Grastorf
10 9 8 7 6 5 4 3 2 1
First Edition
Interior illustration by Ashton Applewhite

Preamble

IN RECENT YEARS the Federal Government and its civil servants have suffered attacks from many quarters. Critics claim that the system does not work. They heap abuse and ridicule on the laws and regulations under which our nation is governed and on those men and women who create and administer them. This collection of letters, memoranda, regulations, and miscellany offers evidence that the critics are wrong. The system is sound, and it works. As E. R. Newman has said, "When governmental operatives interface to paramatize problematical situations, you get soluble overviews every time." This book shows public servants at work, from the highest officeholder to the lowliest career bureaucrat. Borrowed from desks and file cabinets throughout Government, these documents bear testimony to Washington's pursuit of excellence. The book includes items from the Congress, the Departments, and other arms of Government touching upon civil defense, our national heritage, counterintelligence, acts of God, and correct grammer.*

Roger Bruns and George Vogt, career civil servants, have worked overtime to set the record straight. Mostly, the authors let the evidence speak for itself. There is no mess in Washington, and this collection demonstrates just how bad the mess really isn't.

Many years ago, H. L. Mencken likened President Warren G. Harding's prose to a "hippopotamus struggling in a slough of molasses." Another contemporary wrote of those presidential speeches: "They are like vast armies of words moving across the landscape in

---

* Per GSA Form 2892, "Employee Performance Rating and Assessment Relevant to Promotion Potential."

SECTION II - ASSESSMENT OF ABILITIES AND TRAITS RELEVANT TO PROMOTION POTENTIAL					
DIRECTIONS FOR COMPLETING SECTION II The employee must be rated on the first six items. Rate the employee on any of the remaining items for which you have sufficient information to make an evaluation. Supervisors should be rated on all factors. Refer to OAD P 3630.1A, Chapter 3, Part 2, for definitions of assessment ratings.	LESS THAN AVERAGE	AVERAGE	ABOVE AVERAGE	SUPERIOR	UNABLE TO DETERMINE
9. COMMUNICATING IN WRITING - Effectively presenting ideas; persuading others; clarity; proper use of grammer and punctuation; skill in developing reports.				✓	

search of a straggling idea. Once they have found one, they capture it and bear it triumphantly in their midst until it dies of overwork and servitude." This collection of writings and publications demonstrates conclusively just how far forward the Federal establishment has marched in subsequent years.

Governing at Ground Level

"You can always ask for a court injunction."

SGearing:MJMcFadden/ma

Edward H. Levi
Attorney General

January 20, 1976

Sinclair Gearing & Mary Jane McFadden   File: 60-0
Attorneys, Antitrust Division

Vermin, Main Building

    We are reluctant to trouble you with this matter but those in the Division upon whom we must rely for eliminating the below described situation have been ineffective in alleviating our problem.

    The seventh floor of the Main Building is infested with mice and cockroaches. We have not seen rats up here but have seen them in the courtyard and in the bushes surrounding the building. Beginning in September, 1975 when we first came here from the Star Building* we have seen mice scrambling in and out of the fan-cooler units under the windows of several of the offices of the 7600 corridor. Last month one of the secretaries sat down at her desk of a morning, moved a waste basket, and apparently awakened a sleeping mouse. Anyway, she frightened it and it frightened her. It leapt out of the basket and fled to a corner where the only apparent exit is into a ventilator grate. She headed in the opposite direction. Two days ago another secretary arrived in the morning and put her feet under her desk. A mouse ran across them and vanished down an open telephone cable conduit. Work came to a screeching stop that endured some minutes as we poked sticks down the hole and explained the transaction to those whose curiosity had drawn them to the clamor. A similar incident occurred last week. Ms. McFadden left a sandwich in a double-thickness doggy bag on her desk. The next morning, the bag had been gnawed through, the sandwich partially eaten, and the digested remains of that or a previous meal left on the desk

---

* Star is an old (1898) building but better managed than this one. Between 1963 and 1975 there were no mice, no rats, and prompt extermination of occasional outbreaks of cockroaches.

Source: Department of Justice Memorandum

itself and atop official papers superimcumbent thereupon, including one from Senator Eagleton dealing with the Federal Reserve Clearinghouse in Kansas City. Droppings are also routinely found on other desks or the floor. Cockroaches are more frequent. In the jakes I have stomped as many as four at one brief sitting, without even rising from the ceremonial place. Last week, in the evening, three rather large ones emerged from an apparently inedible stack of papers dealing with banks and agricultural legislation as if to keep me company. One escaped by running under my calendar pad, thence off the desk and out of sight. I mashed the other two, one on the obverse of a letter from a congressman and one on the back of Bowie, Rostow, and Bork, "Government Regulation of Business" (Foundation Press 1963). It was with little pleasure that, after washing the remains off my right hand, I contemplated returning to my desk.

I shall forbear narrating the apathy displayed by those we contacted about the matter. Only when Ms. McFadden demanded that something be done in a somewhat hysterical tone did we achieve any response. That response was a GSA employee who left off in her office two paper cupfuls of rat poison, prominently displayed for visitors, opposing counsel, and prospective witnesses to see.

The truth of the matter is that mice and mouse turds are only cutesy-poo in Beatrix Potter books and archie was the only tolerable cockroach in the history of the world. It is demeaning, unprofessional, and unhealthy regularly to associate with rodents and roaches. It is also discouragingly third-worldish to find that a great agency of the United States Government is surrendering to slum fauna in this the two hundredth year of the Republic.

We urge that you direct the appropriate persons to solve the problem forthwith, using whatever emphatic manner of speech is necessary.

"Why don't you pass a law?"

OF MICE AND MEN (AND WOMEN)

Mr. PROXMIRE. Mr. President, I wish to call the attention of the Senate to a problem that faces us all, one of widening dimensions and frightening possibilities. What is this menace that has touched every Senate office with its icy fingers, striking fear into a thousand hearts? What is this plague to good government?

Mr. President, I can sum it up in one word—mice.

Now, I am not just talking about a few mice, a solitary Mickey Mouse or Minnie Mouse. I mean legions of mice that have invaded the Dirksen Office Building and that seem to be moving on the Capitol from many directions.

Mr. President, the great American figure of the last generation did not come out of the golden age of sports. It was not Babe Ruth or Jack Dempsey or Bobby Jones or Bill Tilden or Red Grange. It was not Franklin Roosevelt or Churchill, Hitler or Stalin. It was Mickey Mouse. Sure, Mickey was a creature of the media, but what modern historic figure is not? Mickey was not a joke. He became a way of life. After all, millions of kids were not wearing Red Grange hats or Jack Dempsey or even FDR hats. But they were sure wearing those mouketeer chapeaus.

Mickey and Minnie Mouse are cultural institutions. They took Hollywood by storm, invaded the White House, captured the Nation, and captivated the world. That was all good and fine. But this phenomenon has to stop somewhere. At the present rate, the progeny of Mickey and Minnie Mouse will soon have more voting power than the U.S. Senate. They will dominate the Banking Committee, eat out the cafeteria, control our law making procedures. How long will it be before the majority leader's job is threatened by a mouse coalition?

The majority leader did not hear that, but he ought to be concerned about it, because it could happen. While he is conferring with the minority leader, the mice undoubtedly are moving on all areas of the Capitol.

I once thought there were many different kinds of Republicans—conservative Republicans and liberal Republicans, Northerners and Westerners, big spending and tightfisted Republicans—but they are nothing compared to these mice. We have brown mice, white mice, soft furry mice, spotted mice, short-tailed mice, long-tailed mice, blunt nosed mice, fat, satisfied, arrogant, omnipresent mice. You do not know mice until you have seen one devour a full bowl of poison and look up for more.

Mr. ROBERT C. BYRD. Mr. President, the Senator did not mention the country mouse and the city mouse. Does he know the old story about that?

Mr. PROXMIRE. No, but I would like to hear it.

Mr. ROBERT C. BYRD. Are they involved here?

Mr. PROXMIRE. No, but we have many types of mice and they could include country mice and city mice.

Mr. ROBERT C. BYRD. They were cousins, you know.

Mr. STEVENS. How about arctic mice?

Mr. PROXMIRE. We have arctic mice, Southern mice, Alaskan mice, Wisconsin mice, West Virginia mice. They are eating us up. I can tell you.

Yes, Mr. President, mice—from the sixth floor to the subbasement, behind every radiator, beneath every bookcase—the Dirksen Senate Office Building has been invaded by a marauding battalion of scurrying, foraging rodents. The parade of mice is as long as a New Yorker article about Senator CULVER. It goes on and on and on endlessly.

Mr. ROBERT C. BYRD. Would the Senator suggest that the Pied Piper might be able to get rid of these mice?

Mr. PROXMIRE. We are looking for him. They have a Pied Piper up there, but the poor fellow cannot do much. The mice are taking over. They are leading him.

Mr. ROBERT C. BYRD. Do you suppose I might take my fiddle and lead them away?

Mr. PROXMIRE. It might help. I think a little fiddling might do the trick. It did not work for Nero, but might for the majority leader.

Mr. ROBERT C. BYRD. It worked for Thomas Jefferson. He was a country fiddler.

Mr. PROXMIRE. But he had to cope with rats. We have to cope with mice. The mice are more numerous and they are there.

It began as a small thing—a mouse here, a mouse there. But the problem has grown to epidemic proportions. We can no longer escape it. The mice are everywhere, and their size and number increase daily in geometric profusion.

Mr. ROBERT C. BYRD. If the mice ever join hands with the roaches, what will happen to us then?

Mr. PROXMIRE. Well, I would bet on the mice. I think the mice can do it. The mice have already invaded Hollywood, invaded the White House. Believe me, they are way ahead of the roaches in our

Source: *Congressional Record*, September 15, 1978

office. We have a lot of bullets, but the mice seem to be way ahead.

These mice are a brazen crew, entirely without fear. No room is inviolate, no conference so weighty as to be spared their squeaky presence. They have no morals, no sense of decency. Their presence is an outrage to the dignity of the Congress, an affront to basic human rights everywhere.

This is the age of the mouse.

We have a mouse-like energy bill before us right now. It is not a vicious steal of a bill, but a furtive, timid, gnawing at the public interest. Any self-respecting rat would sneer at it. And I might add that quite a few are doing just that. There is mousiness everywhere. Not only the Congress, but the executive branch and the Supreme Court are not fearsome and tough. All these institutions seem to be made up of a conglomeration of midgets, individually innocuous as a mouse but, in aggregate, as threatening as this army of mice has become.

Take the press. No longer are we plagued with yellow journalism of the ilk of William Randolph Hearst or Bertie McCormick. There are no lions in the press, no wolves. We have to strain even to call them jackals. There are not even any rats in the press, only hundreds of nibbling, on-the-one-hand-on-the-other-hand mice. Take this speech as an example: It had an embargo for Friday, but the release time was broken by AP. Now that is a mousey move if there ever was one. Embargoes, unlike mice, should be honored.

Even organized crime—the classic home of the dirty rat—lacks the class and clout of Al Capone or Lucky Luciano. These days, even the crooks are mousey.

Except for the defense contractors, shipbuilders who are taking rat-sized bites out of the taxpayers, even the rip-offs are more like a gigantic assemblage of mice-nibbles than the spectacular steals of yesteryear.

Sure there are more dollars of waste—more extravagance, more special interest chiseling but it is a problem of too many little marauding rodents each of them harmless but in aggregate nibbling the body politic as never before.

Mr. President, there is only one man, one heroic man, who stands between the Dirksen Building and this marauding horde. One man alone guards this fortress against the nemy.

In its unfathomable wisdom the Senate has hired an exterminator. Every Tuesday night he returns to make his dreary rounds. From office to office, armed with traps and poison, cheese and odor proof plastic bags, he trudges, struggling to stem the endless tide.

Life is cheap for these mice. When our hero returns next Tuesday, grim and determined, another bloody spectacle will await him, another senseless carnage scattered through Senate offices.

Mr. President, what is the explanation for this vicious cycle of slaughter, this ceaseless attrition? Why must this lone crusader return week after week, to endure the screams of frenzied secretaries, to be greeted by the light, acrid stench of decaying mice? Why, Mr. President, why?

I will tell you why.

Like some enormous sponge, like the U.S. Tax Code, like some gargantuan swiss cheese, the Dirksen Senate Office Building is riddled with holes—gaping 3-inch portals pierced by slender 1-inch pipe yawn in every wall, behind every radiator, giving the rodents access to every floor, every room.

And what is the Senate's response to this gross breach of integrity? How have we acted to stem the blight now afflicting this Congress?

With characteristic myopia, we have treated the symptoms while ignoring the causes. We have merely hired one solitary individual, a courageous man but one hopelessly inadequate to rid us of the pest.

Mr. President, how much longer can we wait to attack this problem at its roots? Think of the time lost by Senate employees afraid to return to their offices, having been displaced by thousands of mus musculi. Consider the trepidation of those who fear to open their desk drawers only to face a quickly departing mouse colony. How many mice have secretly typed out a memorandum by random application of their quadrupedal appendages during the night? Could this account for some of our less worthy legislation?

Oh, the irony of this plague. Even now, with one porous Senate Office Building riddled with vermin, another rises up right next door. This lavish structure, the newest Senate Office Building, now rising from the ground almost as fast as its price tag, stands next door to the "holey" Dirksen Office Building, and I mean 'holey.

If we were to take only one ten-thousandth—one ten-thousandth—of the fortune required to build the Hart Senate Office Building, and rather than throw that money down the mouse hole, if we were to take that small sum and plug the holes in the Dirksen Building, I assure you that the results would be startling. We could stuff those holes with dollars and be money ahead. The dollar is not worth much these days. Jamming a few hundred thousand down a mouse hole would be a new and exhilarating change for the Senators from shoveling them down rat holes. No longer would mice scuttle through these fromerly respected halls. The wanton horde that now afflicts the Dirksen Building would quickly recede. There would be so much extra room that we would not have spent over $200 million to build a new edifice. It would be the best investment of the dollar by Congress in years.

Mr. President, I had hoped for Republican support in my efforts to rid the Senate of mice. But the Republicans are running scared. Elephants and mice do not mix, as we all know. Perhaps that is

why there are so few Republicans in the Senate.

This desperate situation cries out for action. Behind the marbled walls of the Dirksen Building there flourishes a mousy Byzantium. Just as the barbarians descended on Rome, this wave of rodents, this pestilence, this Sodom and Gomorrah of the mouse world, now gnaws at the very foundations of the Senate. Unless we act now, the Dirksen Senate Office Building, like Rome, may fall.

Mr. ROBERT C. BYRD addressed the Chair.

The ACTING PRESIDENT pro tempore. The Senator from West Virginia.

Mr. ROBERT C. BYRD. Mr. President, I am encouraged to believe that the epic story of Beowulf, and Oliver, Roland, and King Arthur and all of his knights, Sir Lancelot, Sir Galahad, are about to be relived, as I have listened to this brief and noble speech made by the distinguished Senator from Wisconsin.

He has declared, virtually, a one-man war on mice, and if it were not that I suffered from great trepidations I would seek to join him. But I shall be content with following from afar. I congratulate him.

Just a few days ago I saw a streak. It was not a streaker, it was a streak that went across the floor.

Mr. PROXMIRE. A fully clothed mouse.

Mr. ROBERT C. BYRD. In the Lyndon B. Johnson room. It was one of those mice the Senator was talking about.

So does the Senator know what I did? I got myself a couple of these old-fashioned mousetraps, put a little piece of cheese on it, came in the next morning, the cheese was gone, the trap was sprung—no mouse.

So these mice have developed a technology, I suppose, in this age that has rendered the old-fashioned mousetrap useless.

Mr. PROXMIRE. These mice are smart. We have all kinds and varieties of traps in our office.

Mr. ROBERT C. BYRD. Oh, yes.

Mr. PROXMIRE. We have the old-fashioned traps, we have the new-fashioned traps, we have all kinds of poison. They are not only smart, they are tough. They eat that poison. It makes them stronger and bigger.

Mr. ROBERT C. BYRD. They have a built-in resistance. Their IQ is undoubtedly very high.

Mr. PROXMIRE. It might improve the quality of the Senate as they come on to replace some other kinds.

Mr. ROBERT C. BYRD. May I say in closing, the distinguished Senator from Wisconsin has labored greatly, and what has he brought forth? A mouse.

Mr. PROXMIRE. I thank my good friend, the leader. I thought he was going to ask if I was a man or a mouse. I was going to say that these days I would rather be a mouse. They are winning.

Mr. DANFORTH. Will the Senator yield?

Mr. PROXMIRE. Yes.

Mr. DANFORTH. I would point out, these mice have not only infested the Dirksen Building, they are in the Senate restaurant, as well. The Senator may have wondered what he was eating in the Senate restaurant. Think of what the mice are wondering.

But I wonder, at a time when we can send people to the moon, when the Congress of the United States has such originality and such excellence, why it is beyond our ability and beyond our imagination to be able to build a better mousetrap.

Mr. PROXMIRE. I thank the distinguished Senator from Missouri.

That is the question. As he pointed out so well, he and Senator CHAFEE led the fight on that Hart Office Building. I can understand, that is one of the reasons for it, because they have been driving the mice out of that area into the Dirksen Building.

If we take one ten-thousandth of that money and stuff these holes—the trouble is that Dirksen has a series of holes in every office—and if we stuff them with dollars we would be ahead. The dollar is not worth much. That probably would be the best investment we could make.

I might say, it is good to have Republicans joining in this because I indicated Republican elephants have an aversion to having anything to do with mice.

Mr. HATCH. Will the Senator yield?

Mr. PROXMIRE. Yes.

Mr. HATCH. I am afraid the Republicans, in their characteristic fashion, will bring their elephants in and stamp the mice out, and I think that could have a detrimental effect on our buildings.

I compliment the Senator from Wisconsin for spending so much of the Senate's time on worthwhile merit in comparison to, I would say, 40 percent of the legislation that concerns our time in this Chamber.

I think the Senator will come up with some very extensive, decent, and worthwhile legislation, which we can in a bipartisan effort join to solve this otherwise incredible problem.

The ACTING PRESIDENT pro tempore. The Chair advises Senators that the time for the Mickey Mouse program has expired.

"Or glue Figure 5-6.1 to a brick and throw it at the mouse."

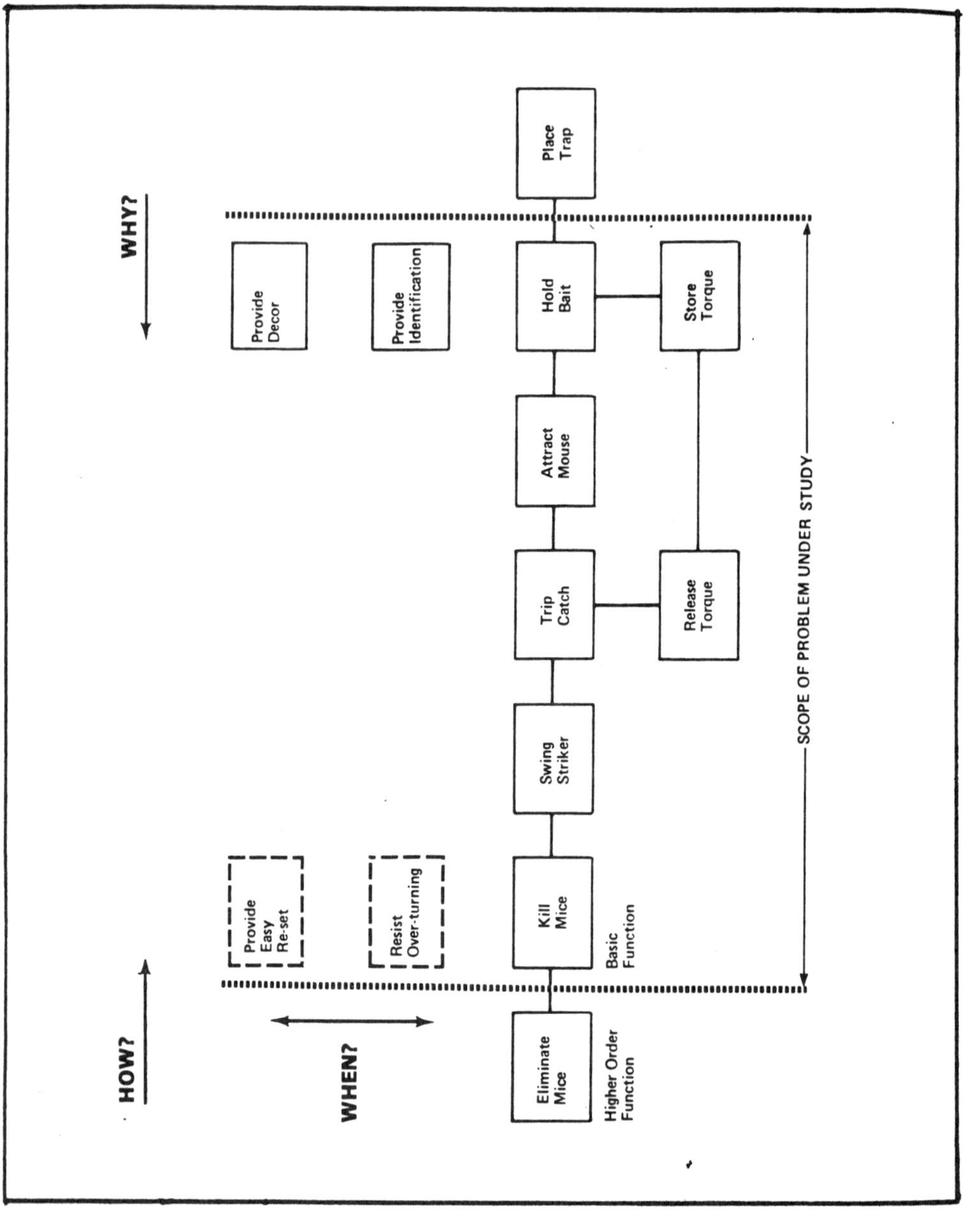

Figure 5-6.1 Mousetrap - FAST diagram

Source: Public Buildings Service Handbook

Getting Off the Ground

"That means 'stand back, big boom.' "

4.6.7.1.1 On-Pad Fire or Explosion

The most serious consequence of an on-pad fire involving the entire Space Shuttle vehicle will be the release of toxic combustion products from the SRB's. The large heat release associated with the burning of the main engine's propellants will assist the cloud of combustion products in rising to a high altitude. Although the quantity of SRB combustion products released at ground level will exceed that released at or near ground level in a normal launch, the additional heat and cloud rise contributed by the main engine's propellants will compensate in terms of ground-level concentrations of hydrogen chloride and chlorine. Analyses of on-pad solid propellant fires have shown that even in the absence of an associated liquid propellant fire, the public emergency exposure limits are not exceeded at ground level. The "worst case" result of an analysis for an SRB fire at the KSC launchsite, using weather data for 1969, was performed by MSFC and is given in table 4-10.

Explosions on the launch pad might achieve significant blast effects under special circumstances. Such circumstances would be those that lead to sudden rupture of the External Tank: Fallback of the Space Shuttle or some gross structural failure of the External Tank or its supports might represent such events. The explosive yield which would result from the hydrogen and oxygen propellants is predicted to be 20 percent. In a worst-case situation, if the explosive yield is taken as 100 percent and an explosion equivalency of 28 kg (61.6 lb) of dynamite per kilogram of hydrogen is used, then the explosion would be equivalent to the detonation of 2.9×10^6 kg (6.3×10^6 lb) of dynamite. The distances to which various adverse effects could be expected are as follows (ref. 4-49).

Effect	Threshold blast wave pressure, N/cm² (psi)	Distance from launch pad, m(ft)
Glass breakage	0.34 (0.5)	4000 (13 000)
Penetrating missiles	1.4 (2)	1500 (5000)
Eardrum rupture	3.4 (5)	800 (2000)
Lung injury	6.9 (10)	500 (1700)
Lethal	21 (30)	300 (1000)

Immediately prior to launch, all unprotected personnel are evacuated from the launch pad. Consequently, no injuries other than to the flight-crew are anticipated, even for this worst-case event.

Source: NASA Environmental Impact Statement

"Please forward my mail to Alpha Centauri."

BEFORE YOU MOVE

Your last few weeks should be filled with the following preparations, as appropriate:

☐ 1. File appropriate forms to have addresses for paycheck, allotments, and bonds changed.

    ☐ SF-1189 — Used to mail paychecks to a bank

    ☐ NASA-52 — Used to mail paychecks to home

    ☐ SF-1192 — Used to change address for U.S. Savings Bonds

    ☐ SF-1198 — Used to change address for savings allotments

☐ 2. Visit your bank, and make arrangements for removing or transferring your funds. Empty the contents of your safety deposit box.

Also, purchase any Traveler's Checks you will be needing. Remember, your personal check is often unacceptable in an area where you are not known. It is wise to carry cash to cover travel and other immediate expenses. Traveler's Checks are considered one of the safest ways to carry cash. (The cost to purchase Traveler's Checks may be reimbursable by the Government.)

☐ 3. You should contact the following places, as appropriate, to arrange a date for the discontinuation of their services and to arrange for the settling of your accounts with them:

Electric company, gas company, fuel company (obtain estimate for value of remaining fuel), telephone company, water company, dairy, bakery, diaper service, laundry and dry cleaner, businesses with which you have accounts, library, and club memberships.

Remember to arrange to keep your telephone <u>connected</u> through moving day.

You will probably have need for it that day.

☐ 4. Arrange for payment of all debts, including close-out utility bills.

☐ 5. Arrange a date to have your major appliances serviced.

Contact a reputable appliance serviceman to arrange a date (preferably 1 or 2 days before your move) to prepare your appliances for shipment.

Your refrigerator, freezer, air conditioner, gas incinerator, automatic washer and dryer, television and antenna, kitchen and attic fans, and stereo system are among the appliances that may need this servicing.

☐ 6. When you have your rugs cleaned, instruct the cleaner to prepare them for shipment.

☐ 7. Take clothes to cleaners and have shoes repaired in time to have them back for packing.

☐ 8. Return library books.

☐ 9. Remove items permanently attached to walls.

☐ 10. Disassemble outdoor gym sets and other apparatuses, as appropriate.

☐ 11. Drain fuel from machinery, such as power mowers, a few days before you move.

☐ 12. Collect things you have loaned to neighbors and return things borrowed.

☐ 13. Empty club lockers.

☐ 14. Be sure to include your children in as many farewell parties as you can.

Source: NASA Employees' Guide for Permanent Change-of-Station Moves

"Bake 3 seconds at distance of 6 feet from launch pad."

The Personalities in Flight Cookbook

MARY HENDERSON

Astronaut John H. Glenn, Jr., beside *Friendship 7*

In combining her hobby of cooking with her vocation in aerospace history, Mary Henderson has succeeded in concocting a surprise treat. The result of this happy and fun mix of recipes from famous air and space personalities like Jackie Cochran, John Northrop, and Neil Armstrong, accompanied by anecdotes, vignettes, and photos, is to bring these high-altitude achievers down to earth and into our homes in a tangible and personal way. Here is a sampling.

John H. Glenn, Jr.
In 1962 John Glenn became the first American to orbit the earth, in the Mercury-Atlas *Friendship 7*. This ground-breaking flight proved that it was necessary to send a man rather than a machine into space to deal with the unforeseen problems of navigation. He later assisted in the Project Apollo planning, specializing in the design and development of the spacecraft and flight control systems. In 1964 he joined the Royal Crown Cola Company and entered politics; in 1974 he was elected senator from the state of Ohio.

James H. Doolittle
WWII hero, air racer and test pilot—"Jimmy" Doolittle's career has spanned five decades of aviation history. He pioneered "blind flying," was in the forefront of the development of 100-octane fuel, led the Tokyo Raid in 1942, and set many speed and distance records. He later commanded the U.S. Eighth Air Force in England. General Doolittle is currently a member of the Board of Directors of Mutual of Omaha.

"Although I hew wood, carry water, and wash dishes, I do not cook and depend entirely upon my favorite girl Joe (my wife) where the preparation of food is concerned."

Mary Henderson is museum technican for the curator of art, National Air and Space Museum.

Annie Glenn's Ham Loaf
six servings

1 pound cured ham, chopped
½ pound fresh ham, chopped
1½ cups dry bread crumbs
2 eggs
¾ cup milk
pepper
¼ cup sugar
¼ cup water
¼ cup vinegar   (over)

July   ca. 150 pp.   50 b&w illus.
6.   paper 515-2 $4.95*

Source: Smithsonian Institution Press Publications Catalog

"A little bottom-heavy, but it might fly."

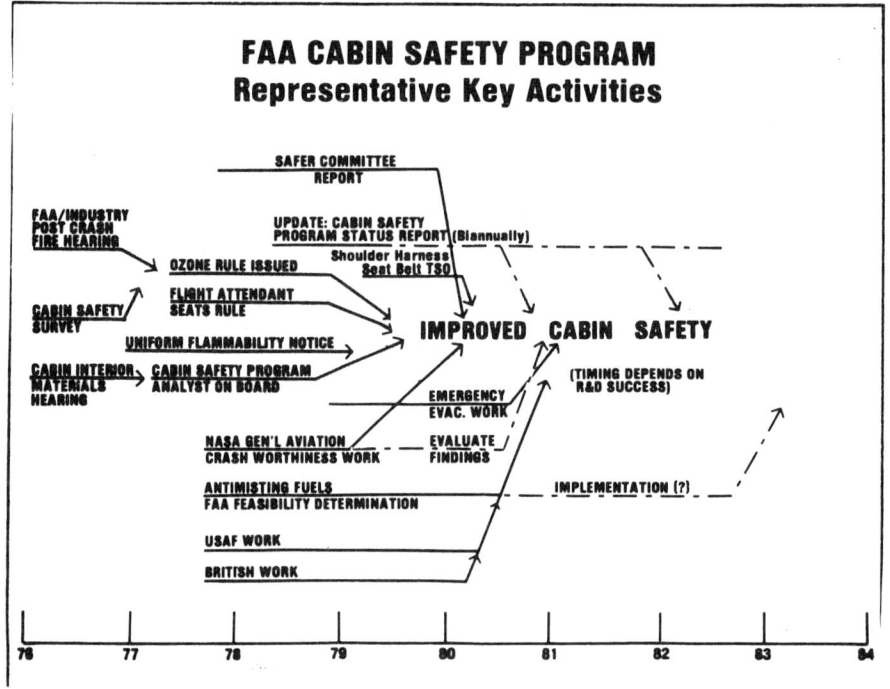

"Send it to Texas, please, COD."

Source: House of Representatives Joint Resolution

96TH CONGRESS
1ST SESSION

H. J. RES. 356

Authorizing the President to proclaim July 1 through July 7, 1979, as "National Sky(lab) Is Falling Week".

IN THE HOUSE OF REPRESENTATIVES

JUNE 7, 1979

Mr. WEAVER (for himself and Mr. EDGAR) introduced the following joint resolution; which was referred to the Committee on Post Office and Civil Service

---

JOINT RESOLUTION

Authorizing the President to proclaim July 1 through July 7, 1979, as "National Sky(lab) Is Falling Week".

Source: Federal Aeronautics Administration Chart

Whereas everything that goes up must come down;

Whereas more than $2,600,000,000 was spent to put Skylab in orbit above the Earth;

Whereas Skylab will be shortly making a spectacular, unscheduled return to Earth which barring liability will be of no cost to the taxpayer;

Whereas with the inexorable increase and proliferation of advanced technology the probability of such unexpected, spectacular occurrences will greatly increase: Now, therefore, be it

Resolved by the Senate and House of Representatives of the United States of America in Congress assembled, That the President of the United States is authorized and requested to issue a proclamation designating the week of July 1 through July 7, 1979, as "National Sky(lab) Is Falling Week", and calling upon the people of the United States to observe such week with appropriate activities, skywatching, and evasive action.

This, the first such spectacular occurrence, a manmade meteor shower covering more than four hundred thousand square miles, consisting of more than five hundred separate pieces, more than half of which will weigh in excess of ten pounds, ten pieces in excess of one thousand pounds, and two pieces in excess of four thousand pounds, all at the mere cost of $2,600,000,000 (plus liability) should be properly observed. Furthermore, it is the sense of the Congress that Skylab should not be permitted to fall in Oregon, where it might mar the natural beauty of that most precious State.

"Better check the bong stockpile, too."

General Services Administration   Office of the Administrator   Washington, DC 20405

Date : May 20, 1980

Reply to
Attn of : The Administrator (A)

Subject : Minutes of Administrator's Staff Meeting - May 20, 1980

To : Heads of Services and Staff Offices
All Regional Administrators

The following was discussed in the above meeting:

- Roy Markon mentioned that audit reports have been issued reporting that ½ ton of opium is missing out of stockpile. He pointed out that opium evaporates and that he is quite comfortable with the security there.

Source: General Services Administration, Minutes of Administrator's Staff Meeting

Raising Standards

"So buy bigger desks!"

UNITED STATES INTERNATIONAL DEVELOPMENT COOPERATION AGENCY
AGENCY FOR INTERNATIONAL DEVELOPMENT
WASHINGTON D C 20523

ASSISTANT
ADMINISTRATOR

OCT 23 1979

Mr. Ray Kline
Deputy Administrator
General Services Administration
18th and F Streets, N.W.
Washington, D.C. 20405

Dear Mr. Kline:

The Agency For International Development has encountered a problem of some proportion which I bring directly to your attention as it will soon obtain in all Executive agencies and doubtless generate costs and embarrassment for the Government if not avoided.

We have found that the new, larger (8½" x 11") standard stationery prescribed by the Joint Congressional Committee on Printing which GSA is stocking for Government-wide use beginning January 1, 1980 is too large to fit the stationery drawers of many standard GSA desks. We discovered that earlier this month when we printed new letterhead necessitated by a recent reorganization, and converted to the larger stationery at the same time to avoid costs of a second conversion three months later.

We have found no single, easy solution of the problem but, rather, have been improvising -- exchanging desks for others in stock, providing desk-top holders and employing other costly devices.

Perhaps the Federal Supply Service can with this advance note of the general problem find some central way to avoid it for the Government as a whole.

Sincerely,

D. G. MacDonald
Bureau for Program and
Management Services

cc: Mr. Boulay, GSA

Source: Agency for International Development

*"**You will have an idea this morning.**"*

October 31, 1978   PBS P 8000.1A

CHAPTER 6. CREATIVITY

1. <u>Introduction</u>. Creativity is the development of ideas new to the individual, not necessarily new to someone else. It is the one element in the methodology that singles out effective VM performance by bringing one closer to the attainment of optimum value. It takes creativity to discover alternate designs, methods, systems or processes that will accomplish the functions that need to be performed.

2. <u>Individual creative capability</u>. Analysis of function through use of creativity is a principal objective of VM, requiring that individuals create on schedule. To some, this challenge seems overwhelming. It is similar to asking one to invent a useful object by noon on Friday of every week. Fortunately, everyone possesses some degree of creative ability. Normally an individual's creative potential is much more than he assumes. As a result, innate creative ability can be developed and improved through training and practice. While there is no precise scientific way of measuring creative action, creative behavior and potential can be subjectively evaluated.

+ Establish a specific time and place for creative thinking.

+ Set a deadline or quotas for creative ability.

+ Write down ideas as they occur.

+ Run over the elements of the problem several times.

+ Take notes on observations.

+ Suspend judgment. Don't jump to or be led into false conclusions.

+ Rearrange the elements of the problem. Get a new viewpoint.

+ Take or break when you are stuck.

+ Discuss your problem with others. Let it incubate.

Figure 6-15. Guide to expanding creative ability

Source: Public Building Service Handbook

"No runs, no hits, and one wrror."

LABOR NEWS DISPATCH
a newsletter of the employees of the national archives
WINNER 1974 NATIONAL AWARD FOR EXCELLENCE
BANNED AT THE NATIONAL ARCHIVES 1978

Vol. VIII, No. 4
February 1980

"On behalf of NARS Management, I wish to apologize for the error which caused a notice from the Administrator regarding GSA policy on sexual harassment to be distributed without a cover sheet prepared by AFGE Local 2578. This erroneous distribution was caused by a communication breakdown with the distribution center. We are confident that such wrrors will not occur in the future."

                                            Charles E. Hall
                                       Personnel Officer, NARS

Source: National Archives Union Newsletter

Making Things Perfectly Clear

"Our God is one God, omnipotent, except as noted in Section 258.24 (b) (1) (ii)."

Federal Register / Vol. 44, No. 208 / Thursday, October 25, 1979 /

Rules and Regulations   61547

Section 258.24   Burden of proof and presumptions.

(b)(1)(ii) *Acts of God.* Several comments raised questions concerning the severity of weather and sea conditions which would qualify as acts of God. Provisions relating to acts of God have been changed in response to these comments. Only weather and sea conditions greater than one standard deviation above the historical mean for the place and season of a casualty will be considered an act of God. Anything less than one standard deviation above the historical mean will be considered a normal operating contingency. The Office of Oceanic and Atmospheric Services of the National Oceanic and Atmospheric Administration will, for each claim which may have been attributable to an act of God, establish the historical mean at the place and season of the casualty, evaluate actual weather and sea conditions at the place and season of the casualty, and decide whether the actual weather and sea conditions were more severe than one standard deviation above the historical mean.

The conditions upon which the presumptions are based are fairly stringent. The presumption for acts of God comes into play only for unusually severe weather and sea conditions. The stringency involved in the presumption for acts of God is necessary to limit compensation for casualties based upon the presumption for acts of God to those consistent with demonstrable probabilities. An act of God may still be established by direct evidence in the event the claimant cannot gain the aid of the presumption. The presumption for casualties attributable to foreign vessels is less stringent. Nevertheless, it is possible for fixed U.S. fishing gear, while unobserved, to be damaged or destroyed by foreign vessels and still not meet the presumption since the Federal Government does not always know the position or activities of all foreign vessels in the FCZ. Since there is no objective way for NMFS to determine whether or not it might be reasonable to believe that an unobserved casualty to fixed U.S. fishing gear was attributable to domestic vessels, no presumption has been established for attributing casualties to the activities of domestic vessels. Thus, all casualties based upon the actions of domestic vessels must be specifically proven.

(4) *Inventory of gear.* Another issue was whether an annual gear inventory should be filed with NMFS as a condition precedent to compensation. This was considered but not adopted because of its potential to produce exorbitant amounts of paperwork for both the program user group and NMFS. It was, instead, determined that an inventory current as of a date immediately preceding the casualty could be submitted along with a claim for compensation.

Accordingly, with the indicated changes, the previously proposed regulations are adopted as set forth hereafter.

Dated: October 22, 1979.

Winfred H. Meibohm,
Executive Director, National Marine Fisheries Service.

Source: National Oceanic and Atmospheric Administration Regulation

"Unless, of course, the Ambassador is held hostage, in which case we will arrange conference calls and revert to the original schedule."

UNCLASSIFIED

STAFF ANNOUNCEMENT

UNITED STATES MISSION - BOGOTA

No.	Subject	Date
78	Chargé's New Meeting Schedule	May 29, 1979

References

TO: All American Employees - All Agencies

FROM: Frank M. Ravndal, Administrative Counselor

The following schedule of weekly meetings will remain in effect until the Ambassador returns in mid-July:

1. The 9:30 a.m. Monday Staff Meeting has been cancelled.

2. A short Staff Meeting will be held every Monday, Wednesday and Friday at 9:00 a.m. in the Ambassador's office for those who normally attend the Tuesday, Wednesday and Thursday 9:00 a.m. meetings.

3. The Military Meeting will be held every Tuesday at 9:00 a.m. instead of every Thursday. The Narcotics Meeting will remain the same - every Tuesday at 9:30 a.m.

4. The Country Team Meeting will be held every Thursday at 9:00 a.m. (instead of Fridays) in the Fourth Floor Conference Room.

DISTRIBUTION "D"

UNCLASSIFIED

Source: Department of State Staff Announcement

"On the other hand, in setting parameters for programmatic responses, downside cost benefit ratios must also be considered."

FACING TOMORROW'S TERRORIST INCIDENT TODAY

HARDENING THE TARGET*

Hardening the target has prophylactic value. It entails denying terrorists access to arms and explosives as well as denying them access to their intended targets. The objective is to make the potential terrorist act so difficult that the amateur is defeated and the professional finds the cost too high. Thus "hardening the target" is synonymous with establishing barriers, some of which are managerial and the others are physical. The physical methods of hardening are to reduce the terrorist's ability to damage a specific installation; and for networks, such as the electric power and communications systems, to increase the number of critical nodes. Here, we consider two types of barriers: (a) denial of means, and (b) security devices and procedures.

On-Line Heuristics

Crisis managers need checklists of "do's and don'ts" in times of strain.* The time for theorizing is over — what decision "rules" can be applied simply to guide government through a dangerous and largely unchartered labyrinth? We lift (in slightly paraphrased form) from the Waterman-Jenkins piece to shed light on the topic.

A heuristic model is a model of a situation stated in terms of heuristics (rules of thumb) which describe the dynamics of the situation. It is particularly useful for problem

---

*The effect of emotional stress on the crisis management team, while providing intense motivation and concentration of effort, can lead to dangerously defective coping reactions. Recent studies of decision-making under emergency conditions have spawned a "conflict" theory of the decision process. (See Janis, I. L. and Mann, L., "Coping With Decisional Conflicts," *American Scientist*, Vol. 64 (Nov-Dec 1976).

The "deduce" action is a signal to process "goals" in an attempt to infer the desired information. The appropriate "goals" would have been constructed by a number of IF . . . THEN relationships that characterize the political-ideology of terrorists.

An example of the deductive inference of GOAL is as follows:

IF: the casualty level of the current-event is "high" or there is a campaign whose event-list is known

&   the name of the current-event is in the event-list of the campaign

&   the frequency of the campaign is "escalating" or the time-between-attacks of the campaign is "short"

THEN: set the public-opinion of the current-event to antiterrorist.

Source: Law Enforcement Assistance Administration Booklet

"Yes, but what's a student?"

COLLEGE OF NAVAL WARFARE
NAVAL WAR COLLEGE
NEWPORT, RHODE ISLAND
02840

CNWNOTE 1301
31/HEC:mlm
16 August 1974

COLLEGE OF NAVAL WARFARE NOTICE 1301

Subj: Assignment of Seminars, Seminar Rooms, Study Rooms and Faculty Teams

Encl: (1) Seminar, Seminar Room, Study Room, and Strategy and Policy Faculty Assignments

1. Purpose. To assign Seminar, Seminar Rooms, Study Rooms, and Strategy and Policy Faculty Teams to College of Naval Warfare students during Academic Year 1974-75.

2. Definitions.

    a. Seminar - A group of about twelve students who will assemble for the purpose discussing a designated subject under the guidance of an assigned Faculty Team.

    b. Seminar Room - A working space assigned to each seminar for regular academic meetings.

    c. Study Room - A working space assigned to students for the purpose of study, research, or other academic endeavors.

    d. Faculty Team - Two or more faculty members assigned to the Strategy and Policy Department who lead seminar sessions with students.

3. Action. Students are requested to review enclosure (1) to determine assignments for the Strategy and Policy Study period.

H. W. SMEVOG
Captain, U.S. Navy
Dean of Students, College
  of Naval Warfare

Distribution:
3, 7a, 7c

Source: Naval War College Memorandum

Writing it Wright

"At first they thought it was just tennis elbow, but when they operated they discovered spreading ego."

Form DOT F 1320.1 (1-67)

UNITED STATES GOVERNMENT

DEPARTMENT OF TRANSPORTATION
OFFICE OF THE SECRETARY

Memorandum

DATE: April 18, 1977

SUBJECT: Correspondence Change for Secretary Brock Adams' Signature

In reply refer to: S-10

FROM: Linda L. Smith *Linda L. Smith*
Executive Secretary

TO: Executive Secretaries
Correspondence Expediters

Because the Secretary has enlarged his signature, we are asking that a minimum of eight spaces be allowed between the complimentary closing and the typed name of Brock Adams on all correspondence prepared for the Secretary's signature. Please refer to the sample below:

Sincerely,

8 spaces between

[signature: Brock Adams]

Brock Adams

This procedure is effective immediately. I would ask that you alert all of the drafting offices within your agency to this change.

In addition I have found that some letters arriving in the Executive Secretariat are typed on the wrong letterhead stationery, with the inside address exceeding the five line limitation and without proper envelopes. Please see that this is corrected. It would also be appreciated if letters addressed to Congressmen and Senators include the room number on the envelope. (See sample below.)

Honorable Harrison A. Williams, Jr.
United States Senate
Washington, D. C. 20510

Russell Bldg. - 352

Source: Department of Transportation

"After infection, the disease spreads rapidly."

COMMITTEE:
VETERANS' AFFAIRS

Congress of the United States
House of Representatives
Washington, D. C.

February 5, 1963

Mr. James Jackson Kilpatrick
Editor
The Richmond News Leader
Richmond, Virginia

Dear Mr. Kilpatrick:

    In view of what is happening today, I took the liberty of placing your excellent editorial of last year in the Congressional Record. A portion of that Record is enclosed.

    The Richmond News Leader is a great newspaper. You are doing a splendid job, and we are proud of you.

    With kindest regards,

    Sincerely,

Wm. Jennings Bryan Dorn, M. C.

D/lm

Source: Kilpatrick Papers, University of Virginia Library

"And, furthermore, Mr. Marcuss wants all work stopped for Good, Friday."

UNITED STATES DEPARTMENT OF COMMERCE
The Assistant Secretary for Industry and Trade
Washington, D.C. 20230

Jack.

CC: Lenz
Scissors
Weiss

September 11, 1979

Roger
Blair
Andy

MEMORANDUM FOR ALL SPECIAL ASSISTANTS

FROM: Jill Feltheimer *Jill Feltheimer*

Stan Marcuss places <u>great</u> importance on correct grammar in all letters he signs, including those for the Secretary or Under Secretary. We will all have to be more careful in the future, <u>especially about commas</u>, which he uses more than <u>the Secretary</u> (but not excessively).

Please be sure to let others in your bureau know. I apologize in advance for any extra work this may cause you, but Marcuss feels very strongly about this.

Source: Department of Commerce

Raising Morale

"Fifty-six crates of bicarbonate of soda to go, please."

FOR IMMEDIATE RELEASE
June 16, 1976

CAKES BAKED FOR BIRTHDAY PARTY

Washington, D.C.—It is the usual thing to do for a birthday party—to bake a cake. But when it is a very special birthday, like the 200th birthday of a nation, cake bakers outdo themselves in concocting the biggest, the best, the most creative cakes they can make. Bakers around the country are doing just that for America's birthday party this July Fourth Weekend.

The biggest, the real superstar of Bicentennial birthday cakes, will be displayed July 3 in Philadelphia's Memorial Hall in Fairmount Park. The five-story-high chocolate cake will be 42 feet across at the base and will weigh in at 49,000 pounds. Produced and donated by the Kitchens of Sara Lee, super-sized layers will be baked, assembled and frosted in the company's New Hampton, Iowa, plant. Decorations, designed at company headquarters in Deerfield, Illinois, will be added to the cake at Philadelphia. The cake and decorations will be transported from Deerfield to Philadelphia in a five-truck convoy, with stops en route to display the scale model.

The red, white and blue cake will be decorated with seals of all the states and territories of the United States, as well as 120 historic scenes from the past, and topped by an American eagle.

A team of pastry chefs, headed by Cornelius (Casey) Sinkeldam, coach of the U.S. Culinary Olympic team, will decorate the colossal chocolate confection. After the festivities, the cake will be disassembled and donated to charitable institutions in the Philadelphia area.

Bicentennial birthday cakes are a citywide effort in Brownsville, Texas. For the last two years, Brownsville youngsters have been collecting and selling cans to recycling plants in order to raise $1,300 for ingredients. And indeed, it is not ordinary birthday cake that will reward them for their efforts. Peggy Quellhorst of Tiffany Bakery is baking 200 sheet cakes, each decorated with a scene from American history. The cakes will be displayed as a patchwork quilt, measuring about 12 by 18 feet, in Brownsville's Amigoland Shopping Mall on July Fourth. A replica of Independence Hall will serve as the centerpiece, and at 6:30 p.m. slices of cake will be served free to the public.

The National Archives will cut a red, white and blue birthday cake at the opening ceremony of a unique tribute to the Declaration of Independence, on July 2. The 36 inch dummy base will be decorated with a huge "Happy Birthday." A two-tier butter pound cake baked and decorated by Buddy Byram of Clement's Bakery of Washington, will feature red, white and blue bunting on the second tier and a large "200" on the top tier. Red, white and blue roses holding American flags will

Source: American Revolution Bicentennial Administration Press Release

decorate the top of the cake. The Archives cake will be cut with an American sword from the Archives' collection and slices will be given to visitors who have filed through the rotunda to view the Declaration of Independence and sign a special guestbook.

At 1:30 on the Fourth the cake will be brought out for serving on the Archives portico, as the U.S. Army Band plays "Happy Birthday."

The Declaration of Independence will be on public view for 76 consecutive hours during the July Fourth Bicentennial Weekend, beginning in the evening of July 2. A military honor guard will stand guard on the Declaration the entire day of July 4.

The Scott County Hospital Ladies Auxiliary will sell slices of cake in Huntsville, Tennessee, as part of Scott County's Bicentennial festivities at noon on July 3 at the county court house. County Judge Verda Cope will choose the favorite cake in this Bicentennial Weekend cake and cookie baking contest.

The *Fantastic Frosters* of Great Falls, Montana are also holding a cake baking contest, specifying that the entires be decorated around the theme of the country's 200th birthday. They plan to feed cake to 2,000 people at the state fairgrounds, as part of Montana's biggest Bicentennial Weekend celebration. Three trophies will be presented to the winners of the individual category and three for commercially baked cakes. At 12:30 on the 4th, the cakes will be judged and at 3 p.m., a fifth grader dressed as Uncle Sam will cut and serve the first prize cake. And, of course, the whole community will sing "Happy Birthday, America."

In Champaign, Illinois, the entire population is being invited to bring a birthday cake to the open area across from the University of Illinois football stadium after the Fourth of July parade. Bicentennial themes are expected to dominate the cake decorations. Also, the Eisner's Grocery Store will provide a large birthday cake to be given away at the evening's festivities, which will end with a fireworks display in the stadium.

The Baltimore Bicentennial Committee is selling 400,000 slices of Bicentennial birthday cake ($2.25/slice) to finance historic restoration projects in the city. A plywood dummy cake in the shape of the continental United States will contain frosted, pre-wrapped slices of butter pound cake in souvenir Bicentennial boxes.

At midnight on July 3, the 50 by 20 by 8 feet cake will be floated on a barge from Baltimore's Inner Harbor to Ft. McHenry, where the barge will be docked and 200 electric candles will be lighted. Herman's Bakery in Baltimore has been baking 1,000 pounds of cake per day since the first of June. The frozen cakes are being shipped to Philadelphia for wrapping and packaging, then shipped back for the Bicentennial Weekend celebration in Baltimore.

In the dummy cake category, Frances Nave of the Wright Bakery in Johnson City, Tennessee, will produce a large "cake" sporting 200 candles which will be placed on an old-time wagon as part of the July Fourth parade in Jonesboro, Tennessee. Jonesboro, the oldest town in Tennessee, has just completed a two-year renovation project, and its "Historic Jonesborough Days" celebration during the Bicentennial Weekend is expected to draw upwards of 100,000 visitors. Mrs. Nave's cake float will feature red, white and blue liberty bells and '76 flags.

A three-story-high dummy Happy Birthday America cake is the finale of Hooray U.S.A., a special Bicentennial extravaganza opening July 4 at the Miami Beach Convention Center. The production follows major historical periods beginning with July 4, 1776, and ending with the 1969 landing on the moon.

As the final song is sung, the giant red, white and blue "cake" is rolled out to the center of the hall, lighted by 200 electric candles, and the whole house sings "Happy Birthday America."

Whether pretend or real, colossal or cupcake size, commercial or home baked, Bicentennial birthday cakes are one example of the many kinds of tributes present day patriots are paying to the United States of America on its 200th anniversary.

"All the news that's fit to print."

THE LINK

Vol. 1, No. 2
April 1980

Wake Up, Everybody, It's Spring!

Spring has finally descended on Washington. The wet, cold, seemingly endless winter has passed. In its wake are longer and warmer days, sunshine, fragrant blossoms, birds, kites, and--generally speaking--a good number of happier people. It is a time of reflection, of a search for new beginnings; a time of new life, of rebirth--and of taking advantage of the 5/4-9 work schedule!

For those of us here at OJARS, LEAA, BJS and NIJ, the winter has been a most anxious one. Concerns of reauthorization and reorganization; of future program efforts; of budget cuts... Despite these anxieties, however, most employees--to their everlasting credit--have maintained their spirits, many with a healthy amount of good humor.

So it was discovered as we wandered about the agency on the first day of spring, asking co-workers: <u>Just what does spring mean to you?</u>

The answers? Well, they're different! Here are some of them.

Many of us saw the practical side of spring. Said one OJARS official, "Spring means my heating bill will go down $100 per month!" This sentiment was echoed by many.

Several employees said spring meant "new clothes," "throwing away my winter coat," and "wearing brightly colored and lighter clothing."

Tom Madden, OGC, quipped to a LINK reporter: "Spring? Why, spring means a change of seasons." Thoughtful.

Malcolm Barr, PIO, said, "Spring symbolizes the onset of my annual bout with insomnia. Stirrings in the old breast, of course." Typically British.

Ralph Muros and Mike Cronin were approached at the same time with the question. Ralph said, "Spring means that all the saps are rising."

Mike said spring made him sympathetic to baseball players. "It's really a hard time for them. They have to play an extra hour each game to go with the longer days, you see." Bureaucratic.

One LEAA voice welcomed spring because it brings "good job hunting weather." Optimistic.

To Jay Brozost, spring means "it's a little bit hotter and a little bit more crowded at the Capitol Hill Club." Pessimistic.

"Spring means getting outdoors," said Allen Benson, OCJP. That's what all the jocks say.

Bob Aserkoff, OCJP, responded to the question with a song. "Spring--flowers blooming, children singing, for me and my girl, la-di-da-di-da." Huh?

The LINK award for the most enlightening comment is presented to what we'll call the "Terrible Trio" in the Corrections Division--three women who refused to be identified. Pulling a remake on the popular girl-watching theme, the "Trio" said spring meant "all the hunks with big legs will be out jogging in L'Enfant Plaza in their shorts!" Right on.

Have a happy spring!

Say "Thank You" to Your Secretary

National Secretaries Week   April 21-25

Source: Department of Justice Newsletter

"Wanted: Experienced second baseman. Teeshirts provided."

GENERAL SERVICES ADMINISTRATION
WASHINGTON, D. C. 20405

ADM 527
January 9, 1979

GSA NOTICE

SUBJECT: GSA Choir

Since becoming Administrator, I have strongly supported the use of art in the Federal buildings, such as the Art in Architecture Program. Music is also a form of art, and I wish to encourage its use by establishing the GSA Choir which is to be composed of interested GSA employees. The Choir will perform at official functions, at Christmas, at a spring concert, and at various other times throughout the year. Choir rehearsal will be held on every Tuesday from 11:30 a.m. to 12:30 p.m. in the GSA auditorium. Interested members will be notified of the first Choir practice.

Alene Vaughn, one of my confidential assistants, will direct the choir. Alene has had many years of musical training and experience in choir direction.

If you are interested in singing in the choir or in auditioning for piano accompanist, please complete the attached form and send it to room 6137.

JAY SOLOMON
Administrator

Name: Correspondence symbol:

Phone: Voice part:
                                  ( ) Soprano   ( ) Alto
                                  ( ) Tenor   ( ) Base
                                  ( ) Do not know

( ) I wish to audition for the piano accompanist. (An alternate also
    will be chosen.)

Return to Alene Vaughn, room 6137.
Should you have any questions, please call Alene Vaughn at 566-1212.

Distribution: EEDC; 3GDC; 3WDC
GSA DC-01902003

Source: General Services Administration Notice

Disaster Planning

"Pardon me, is this the parcel post line or the post-attack registration line?"

CSCEL A- 103 (1)

UNITED STATES CIVIL SERVICE COMMISSION

WASHINGTON 25, D. C.

November 13, 1962

CSC EMPLOYEE LETTER A-103
(Supersedes CSC EL B-115)

TO ALL EMPLOYEES

SUBJECT: Nationwide Post-Attack Registration of Federal Employees

Each one of us, as citizens and Federal employees, has a responsibility to contribute to the strength of our Nation. Just as we as individuals must work out plans for ourselves and our families in an emergency, so also must our Government maintain plans to make sure it can continue to operate even in the event of an attack on this Country.

Many Commission employees have specific responsibilities and instructions regarding relocation in the event of a national emergency. Those of you who have such a relocation assignment have been formally notified. At the same time, many of you do not have specific assignments in the Commission's emergency staffing plan. However, all Commission employees, with or without specific emergency assignments, should be fully aware of the nationwide post-attack registration system for Federal employees.

In the event of an emergency brought about by an attack on this Country, the Civil Service Commission will operate a registration system for Federal employees in affected areas. The procedure for this system is as follows:

> If you are prevented from going to your regular place of work because of an enemy attack -- or if you are prevented from reporting to any emergency location -- keep this instruction in mind -- <u>go to the nearest Post Office, ask the Postmaster for a Federal employee registration card, fill it out and return it to him</u>. He will see that it is forwarded to the office of the Civil Service Commission which will maintain the registration file for your area. After the card is received, decision will be made as to where and when you should report back for work. There is another important reason why you should mail in a registration card as soon as you can do so -- this card will also enable us to keep you on the roster of active employees, and enable us to forward your pay.
>
> You should obtain and <u>complete the registration card as soon after enemy attack as possible</u> but not until you are reasonably sure where you will be staying for a few days. If

Expiration Date: <u>Indefinite</u>

Source: Civil Service Commission

"For short fuses, skip from 3c to 5c."

**FOREIGN SERVICE INSTITUTE
DEPARTMENT OF STATE**

TERRORISM: AVOIDANCE AND SURVIVAL

BOMB THREAT REPORT FORM

Date: _____ Time: _____

1. Name of Recipient: _____

2. Exact words of threat: _____

3. Questions to ask:
   a. WHEN will the bomb explode?
   b. WHERE is the bomb located?
   c. WHAT kind is it and what does it look like?
   d. WHY are you threatening us?

4. Identification of the Caller (circle appropriate words):—

   IDENTITY: Male Female Adult Child

   VOICE: Loud Soft High Deep Pleasant Drunk
   Harsh Raspy

   ACCENT: Yes No English Foreign Local Unfamiliar

   SPEECH: Fast Slow Clear Slurred Stutter Calm
   Excited Angry Scared Nasal Lisp

   LANGUAGE: Good Poor Dirty Educated Slang

   BACKGROUND NOISE: Office/Factory Street/Traffic
   Trains/Airplanes Party Atmosphere Quiet/Arguments

5. Other helpful information:
   a. Did the caller appear familiar with residence or building by the description of the location of the device?
   b. Could the call be made from a phone booth?
   c. Other Comments.

REMEMBER: THERE ARE NO RULES OR LINES OF DIF-FERENTIATION BETWEEN A HOAX CALL AND THE REAL THREAT.

9

Source: Department of State Foreign Service Institute Booklet

"How about a giant cork?"

II CONGRESS
1ST SESSION

H. R. 7771

IN THE HOUSE OF REPRESENTATIVES

JUNE 14, 1977

HEFTEL introduced the following bill; which was referred to the Committee on Public Works and Transportation

A BILL

To control volcanic activity.

Be it enacted by the Senate and House of Representatives of the United States of America in Congress assembled, That section 5 of the Flood Control Act approved August 18, 1941 (33 U.S.C. 701n) is amended by inserting at the end thereof the following: "The Chief of Engineers is also authorized to accomplish advance measures using amounts in the emergency fund, when in his discretion local and State efforts are unable to complete emergency work for control of lava flow, in order to provide the minimum necessary **protection** to prevent loss of life and damages to improved **property** when such volcanic activity can be predicted or reasonably anticipated.".

I

"A silver lining in every mushroom cloud."

The Effects of Nuclear War

CONGRESS OF
THE UNITED STATES
Office of Technology Assessment
WASHINGTON, D. C. 20510

Long-Term Effects

Postattack society would be permanently and irrevocably changed. People would live in different places, work at different jobs, and travel in different ways. They would buy different things and take different kinds of vacations. The Nation would tend to apply the lessons of the past to future policy by seeking to reduce its vulnerabilities to the last attack. Energy conservation, where not required by regulations, would be encouraged by prices, taxes, and subsidies. Railroads and mass transit would supplant travel by cars and planes; rail and ships would substitute for planes and trucks in hauling freight. Automobile production would drop sharply and would emphasize energy-efficient models; bicycles and motorcycles would be popular. While housing construction would not necessarily end in the suburbs, new homes there would probably be built closer together so that mass transit could serve them. Construction in cities would boom. All houses would be better insulated; more would use solar energy as fuel costs soared.

The Nation's adjustment to all these changes would be painful. The problems would be especially severe because of the speed of their onset. Many people say that the United States would be better off if it was less dependent on cars and petroleum. While changing to new patterns of living via nuclear attack would minimize political problems of deciding to change, it would maximize the difficulties of transition. Problems would appear all at once, while any advantages of new patterns of living would come slowly.

Source: Office of Technology Assessment Booklet

"In an emergency, you may eat the telephone. Rest assured that someone, somewhere, will eventually notice your absence."

CSC EL B-228

U. S. CIVIL SERVICE COMMISSION

WASHINGTON, D. C. 20415

November 6, 1963

CSC EMPLOYEE LETTER B-228

TO ALL CENTRAL OFFICE EMPLOYEES

SUBJECT: Instructions for employees who may be on stalled elevators

On a few occasions since we moved, some of our employees have been on elevators when they became stuck between floors. The inconvenience and distress this has caused employees is unfortunate, and we naturally hope these situations will not arise again. However, bearing in mind that the elevators are new and that some mechanical adjustments still may be necessary, we would like to give this advice to all employees in the event they are on an elevator that becomes stalled.

There is a telephone in each elevator. Each telephone is recessed in the wall, behind a small door, at the front of the elevator. There is an instruction sheet on the front of the door, which gives telephone numbers of the elevator mechanic and the guard. In the event of elevator failure, all you need to do is use the elevator telephone and dial the number for the elevator mechanic--or the guard if the elevator mechanic's number does not answer--and report that the elevator is stuck.

Each elevator also is equipped with an emergency lighting system which should automatically provide light in the elevator in the event of power failure. We understand this lighting system did not work recently when normal power failed in one of the elevators. The mechanics are checking the system to assure that it works in all our elevators.

Above all, do not panic if you are caught in a stalled elevator. There is no cause for alarm. Remain calm until the elevator mechanics restore power and return the elevator to service.

Expiration Date: Indefinite

Source: Civil Service Commission Directive

Liberating the Ladypersons

"The owner, she is not amused."

The Starting-and-Managing Series • Vol. 14

STARTING AND MANAGING A
CARWASH

SMALL BUSINESS ADMINISTRATION

Your Team

The size of the team you will be managing will depend on the size and type of operation you set up. A typical carwash might have—in addition to the owner-manager—a "front man," an assistant manager, the wash-line crew, and a cashier.

The "front man." Every organization needs a front man. At first, you will probably fill this slot. Later, as your business grows, you may hire an employee to do the job. The front man is the one who deals directly with the customer. He is the salesman of your services. This is the person who will promote your carwash to fleet operations, to new- and used-car dealers. He is the man who will handle most contacts with all customers—their complaints, their problems. Probably he will also be directly involved in your advertising and public-relations programs.

Source: Small Business Administration Manual

The cashier. Your cashier is one of the most important persons in your plant. Often she acts as a part-time bookkeeper. At the least, she is responsible for the daily tabulation of carwash tickets and for credit-card slips if you honor such cards.

She may also handle merchandise sales. As the person with the most direct contact with your customers, she's the natural one to sell your waxing, polishing, and reconditioning services. She's the closest thing you'll have to a salesman inside your plant and she should be alert to sales possibilities with every customer.

A pleasant personality and a friendly smile are musts for your cashier. She's in a position to win more friends for your carwash in an hour than the rest of your employees—including your manager—can make in a week.

Interiors. Women are more particular about the interiors of their cars than most men are. They are quick to complain when they see a trail left by the swipe of a damp cloth across the dashboard—one clean streak with thick dust everywhere else. They also resent not having the ashtrays emptied. Many carwashes don't empty ashtrays because of the time it takes. Or they don't want to risk doing some damage if the ashtray is hard to remove (it sometimes is). Other carwashes provide litter barrels along the outside of the carwash where the cars wait in line. Signs on the barrels ask the motorists to empty their own ashtrays.

"Tell it to a Gerperson and duck."

presidential documents

Title 3—The President

PROCLAMATION 4524

Leif Erikson Day, 1977

By the President of the United States of America

A Proclamation

Once again it is appropriate for Americans to honor the intrepid Norse explorers who overcame hardship and adversity to reach our shores so long ago.

The United States is a young Nation, but our debt to that courageous Norseperson, Leif Erikson, predates 1776 and recalls a distant age when brave adventurers sailed forth into the unknown. As a people we continue to embody this spirit of bold discovery, and we take pride in his historical exploits.

As a mark of respect for Leif Erikson and the Norse explorers, the Congress of the United States, by joint resolution approved September 2, 1964 (78 Stat. 849, 36 U.S.C. 169c), authorized the President to proclaim October 9 in each year as Leif Erikson Day.

NOW, THEREFORE, I, JIMMY CARTER, President of the United States of America, do hereby designate Sunday, October 9, 1977, as Leif Erikson Day and I direct the appropriate Government officials to display the flag of the United States on all Government buildings that day.

I also invite the people of the United States to honor the memory of Leif Erikson on that day by holding appropriate exercises and ceremonies in suitable places throughout our land.

IN WITNESS WHEREOF, I have hereunto set my hand this twenty-third day of September, in the year of our Lord nineteen hundred seventy-seven, and of the Independence of the United States of America the two hundred and second.

Jimmy Carter

[FR Doc.77-28570 Filed 9-26-77;10:27 am]

FEDERAL REGISTER, VOL. 42, NO. 187—TUESDAY, SEPTEMBER 27, 1977

Source: Presidential Proclamation and *Congressional Record*, September 30, 1977

ORWELLIAN ERA IS UPON US

(Mr. MICHEL asked and was given permission to address the House for 1 minute and to revise and extend his remarks.)

Mr. MICHEL. Mr. Speaker, I dare say the Orwellian era is upon us. It was George Orwell, you will remember, who gave us "1984" and those descriptive examples of how history was constantly being rewritten to suit the whims of Big Brother.

Orwell's State of Oceania is alive and well within our shore. History is being rewritten by the White House. How else can you account for President Carter's proclamation, quoted in the Washington Post the other day, which decrees that Leif Ericson was not in fact a Norseman. The President has declared that Ericson and all his countrymen, excuse me, countrypersons, were Norsepersons.

If this is indeed a sign that history is being rewritten, I must express grave concerns. What is it going to cost to rewrite all those history books and reprogram those of us already educated in the old-fashioned way of doing things?

I think our President ought to explain this new application of his power. He is ultimately responsible. One of his first actions as President was to proudly display on his desk a reminder that "the buck stops here," a reminder first made famous by that great leader and great President, Harry S. Truperson.

"Would the longshoreworker who left his or her purse in the ladies' room please claim it from the foreperson at lunch."

UNITED STATES DEPARTMENT OF COMMERCE
The Assistant Secretary for Administration
Washington, D.C. 20230

MEMORANDUM FOR   HEADS OF ALL OPERATING UNITS

SUBJECT: Gender-free Terminology

In my prior memorandum on this subject dated August 14, 1978, I recommended that the <u>1977 Dictionary of Occupational Titles</u> be the reference source for checking sex-specific job titles. I used as an example the terms: *stevedore* and *longshoreman*, and stated in a footnote that since *longshoreman* did not appear in the <u>Dictionary</u>, *stevedore* should be used in its stead.

It has come to my attention that, contrary to the contention of the authors of the <u>Dictionary</u>, *stevedore* and *longshoreman* are not the same job.1/ Therefore, please advise your employees that the term *longshoreman* may be used when necessary to interpret the provisions of a statute. Otherwise, *longshore worker* is the preferred gender-free term.

It remains the policy of the Department of Commerce to replace gender-specific terms with non-sexist language whenever possible. Our intent is to use gender-free job titles where alternative titles exist, not to alter the substance of jobs. Although the <u>1977 Dictionary of Occupational Titles</u> appears to have erred with respect to this particular job, it shall remain the general reference for checking job titles.

Elsa A. Porter
Assistant Secretary
for Administration

1/ A *stevedore* is an employer who is responsible for the loading and unloading of ships. A *longshoreman* is an employee (of the stevedore) who actually loads and unloads ships. The International Longshore Association informs us that its female workers are called "longshoremen."

RECEIVED 4/17/79

Source: Department of Commerce

Teaching the Masses

"Next, try it with bananas in each ear."

THIS SIDE UP

Making Decisions About Drugs

National Institute on Drug Abuse
Office of Communications and Public Affairs
5600 Fishers Lane
Rockville, Maryland 20857

U.S. DEPARTMENT OF HEALTH, EDUCATION, AND WELFARE
Public Health Service
Alcohol, Drug Abuse and Mental Health Administration

Source: National Institute on Drug Abuse Booklet

TAKE A MIND TRIP

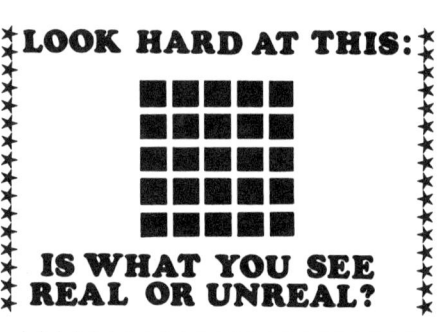

A mind trip is a way to feel high without drugs. Take one of the mind trips below by yourself or with some friends.

Sonata for Oven Rack

All you need for a journey to stereo heaven is:
- One oven rack (or refrigerator rack if your oven rack is too grubby to associate with).
- Two pieces of string, about 3 to 4 feet in length.
- One or two friends, about 5 feet in length.
- A bunch of assorted kitchen utensils, like a wooden spoon, soup ladle, wire whisk, fork, etc.

Tie one end of each string to a corner of the rack as shown. (An illustration has been thoughtfully provided for you.) Now take the free ends of each string and wind around the top part of each index finger. Four or five wraparounds will do. Insert your fingers (gently) into your ears.

At this point your assistants should start playing the rack by striking it with the kitchen utensils or their hands. All they will hear is a lot of clanging. The sounds you'll hear are a delight. It's as if you've shrunk to about 6 inches tall and are doing a tumbling routine inside a grand piano!

★★★★★★★★★★★★★★★★★★★★★★
LOOK HARD AT THIS:

IS WHAT YOU SEE REAL OR UNREAL?
★★★★★★★★★★★★★★★★★★★★★★

"Now, where can I buy some?"

FOR PARENTS ONLY:

WHAT YOU NEED TO KNOW ABOUT MARIJUANA

U.S. DEPARTMENT OF HEALTH, EDUCATION, AND WELFARE
Public Health Service
Alcohol, Drug Abuse, and Mental Health Administration

National Institute on Drug Abuse
5600 Fishers Lane
Rockville, Maryland 20857

Marijuana Jargon

Parents today are trying to cope not only with marijuana but also with the drug's vocabulary. While drug terms are continually changing and are often different in various parts of the country, this list may help you decipher the most popular marijuana jargon.

Acapulco Gold—a potent strain of marijuana with gold or yellow highlights.

Bong—a cylindrical water pipe used to smoke marijuana.

Burn out—a slang term for a state of apathy and deadened perceptions which can result from habitual use of marijuana.

Buzz—slang term for a high or a drug-induced euphoria.

Colombian—a potent strain of marijuana.

Decriminalization—process of reducing penalties for personal use of marijuana from prison sentences to civil fines.

Dime—a quantity of drugs which sells on the streets for $10.

Dope—slang term for marijuana and other drugs.

Duster—cigarette made of tobacco, mint leaves, marijuana, or parsley sprinkled with phencyclidine (PCP), also known as Angel Dust.

Ganja—a potent form of *Cannabis* obtained from the flowering tops and leaves of the plant. It may also be used to refer to marijuana in general.

Grass—slang term for marijuana.

Hashish—a form of *Cannabis* made either from the *Cannabis sativa* plant or its resin.

23

Source: Department of Health, Education and Welfare: Public Health Service Booklet

43

Hash oil—a form of *Cannabis* which is extracted or distilled from the *Cannabis sativa* plant.

Head shops—stores which specialize in the sale of drug paraphernalia and drug-related items.

High—a widely used slang term for euphoria and intoxication.

Hit—a single drag or inhalation of marijuana smoke.

Joint—a hand-rolled marijuana cigarette.

Killer weed—slang term for PCP-treated parsley or marijuana.

Loaded—slang term for state of being high or intoxicated.

Nickel—a quantity of marijuana which sells on the street for $5.

Ounce—a standard unit of measurement for marijuana.

Paraphernalia—drug equipment or gadgets usually sold in head shops.

Pot—slang term for marijuana.

Reefer—slang term for marijuana.

Roach—the small end of a marijuana joint which remains after most of the cigarette is smoked.

Roach clip—a device used to hold the roach or the tail end of a marijuana joint.

Rolling papers—cigarette papers used to make a marijuana joint.

Scales—paraphernalia used to weigh drug quantities for selling purposes.

Smoking stones—paraphernalia used to hold marijuana joints while smoking.

Space cadet—slang term for a habitual marijuana user whose senses have become dulled.

Spaced out—slang term for a drug-induced state of being lost or out of touch with surroundings.

Stash—Any container or place used to store marijuana or other drugs.

Stoned—slang term for being high or intoxicated from marijuana.

Supergrass—slang term for marijuana treated with phencyclidine (PCP or Angel Dust).

Toke—slang term for an inhalation of marijuana or hashish smoke.

Water pipe—paraphernalia used to smoke marijuana or hashish which filters the smoke through water.

Weed—slang term for marijuana.

"They left out macaroni bushes and nauga farms!"

CHRONOLOGICAL LANDMARKS IN AMERICAN AGRICULTURE

United States
Department of
Agriculture

Economics,
Statistics,
and Cooperatives
Service

Agriculture
Information
Bulletin No. 425

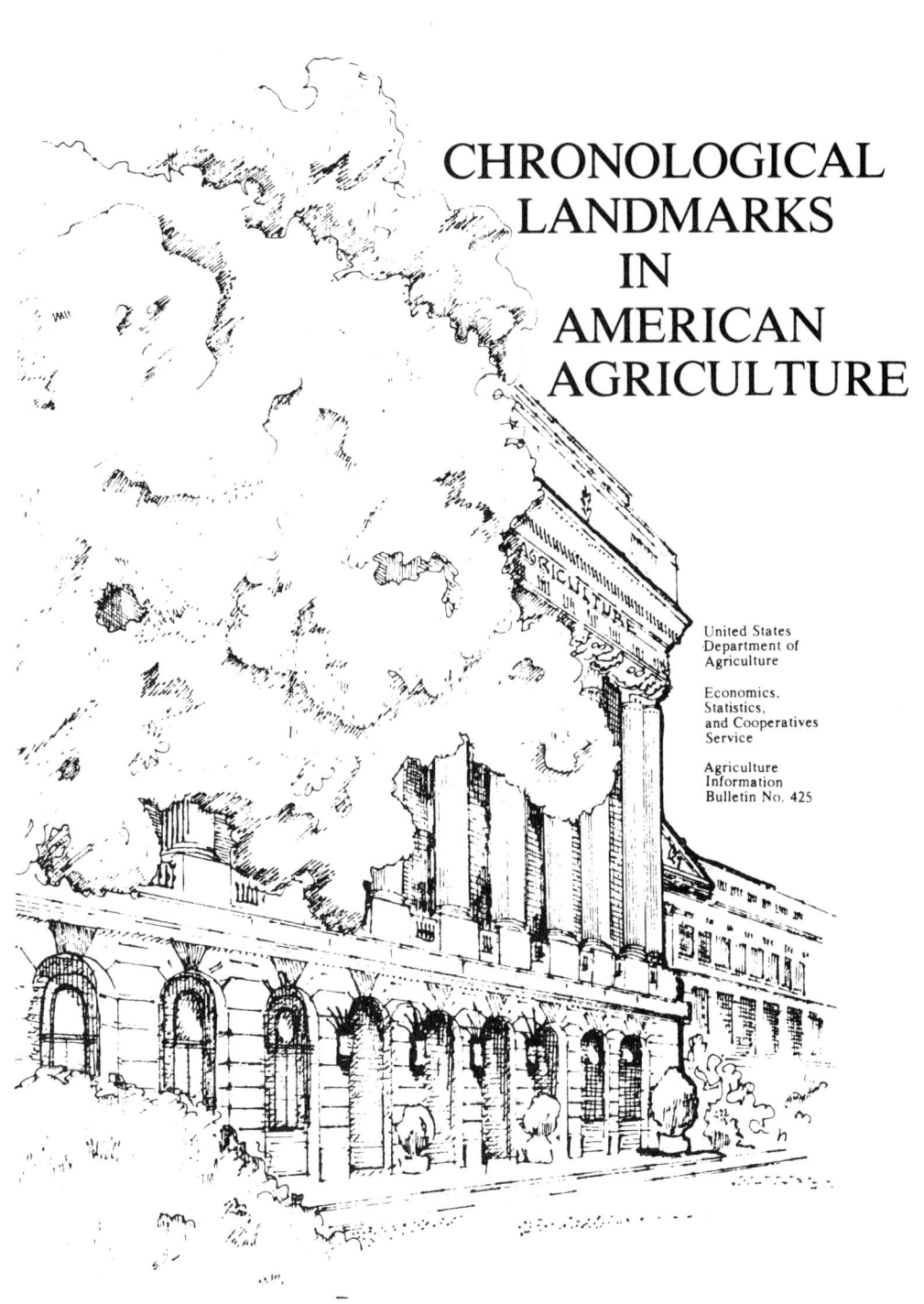

Source: Department of Agriculture Bulletin

45

CHRONOLOGY

8000 B.C. Animals were tamed and grain was domesticated in the Middle East. (Wayne D. Rasmussen, "Valley to Valley, Country to Country," Yearbook of Agriculture, U.S. Dept. Agr., 1964, pp. 1-11.)

1776, July 4. The Declaration of Independence was proclaimed.

1801. The refrigerator was invented by Thomas Moore of Maryland. (Oscar Anderson. Refrigeration in America: A History of a New Technology and Its Impact. Princeton, N.J.: Princeton University Press, 1953. 344 pp., index.)

1846, September 10. A patent for a sewing machine was taken out by Elias Howe. In 1850, a competitor, Isaac M. Singer, marketed the first practical machine with interchangeable parts in the United States. (Ruth Brandon. A Capitalist Romance: Singer and the Sewing Machine. Philadelphia, Pa.: J. P. Lippincott Co., 1977. 244 pp., index, biblio.)

1870. Foot-and-mouth disease was first reported in the United States. (Manual A. Machado, Jr., "Aftosa and the Mexican-United States Sanitary Convention of 1928," Agricultural History 39:240-245. Oct. 1965.)

1874. The pressure cooker was invented. Patents were first granted in 1902, although pressure cookers were not/in general use until 1935. (G. E. Hilbert, "Better Ways of Handling Food," Yearbook of Agriculture, U.S. Dept. Agr., 1954, pp. 128-132.)

1912, August 24. The parcel post system was established by act of Congress. (Gerald Cullinan. The Post Office Department. New York, N.Y.: Frederick A. Praeger. 19__ 272 pp., index.)

1914, August 1. World War I began in Europe.

1955. The National Cowboy Hall of Fame was chartered to preserve the heritage of the West. It marked the fruition of a lengthy one-man crusade by Chester A. Reynolds of Kansas City. (A. M. Gibson, "The National Cowboy Hall of Fame," Agricultural History 33:103-106. July 1959.)

1926. Research was started by the DuPont Laboratories on nylon, although commercial production did not begin until 1938. (Bernice M. Hornbeck, "Fibers Made by Man," Yearbook of Agriculture, U.S. Dept. Agr., 1964, pp. 258-260.)

"Try a giant can opener."

CRASH VICTIM EXTRICATION TRAINING COURSE
EMERGENCY MEDICAL TECHNICIAN

STUDENT'S MANUAL

U.S. DEPARTMENT OF TRANSPORTATION
NATIONAL HIGHWAY TRAFFIC SAFETY ADMINISTRATION
EMERGENCY MEDICAL SERVICES

Source: National Highway Traffic Safety Administration Student's Manual

Surveying the Scene

Now I'm starting to get a better idea of what an accident can involve.

Good! Now let's consider a few things that you should look for when you get there. In fire fighting talk, we would call this sizing up the situation.

Chapter Four Extrication Considerations (or the art of metal bending)

Gaining Entry

Things to think about in answering this question are: Why won't the door open? Is it locked? Or, is the body sprung out of shape, wedging the door shut? Answers to these questions will lead to a solution to the problem. Remember one of the general rules required us to tackle the easiest problems before taking on the big ones. Without a doubt, the easiest way to get into a car is through the door. The door also provides a large opening to exit with a very bulky package. Next to the door, a window would probably be the preferred method of entry. Finally, if neither of these alternatives is possible, you will be forced to gain entry by cutting through some metal. Obviously, this will be somewhat more difficult and time-consuming than the other two methods.

But let's go back and take a look at the door again. If it is only locked, then we can simply unlock it and proceed. Since we don't have a key, and assuming those inside are unable to assist us, one method of gaining entry would be to break out a window and then simply lift the locking button by hand or with a tool which can grip it. If you use your hand, be sure that you have your gloves on!

Establishing Control

I can see why it takes a certain type of person to perform effectively in the midst of all of the confusion at an accident scene.

You're right, but the old leadership adage can be paraphrased, and it applies: extricators are made, not born.

Toiling on the Hill

"How about old gunslingers from California?"

94TH CONGRESS
1ST SESSION

H. J. RES. 673

IN THE HOUSE OF REPRESENTATIVES

SEPTEMBER 29, 1975

Mr. JACOBS introduced the following joint resolution; which was referred to the Committee on the Judiciary

JOINT RESOLUTION

Proposing "The Better Part of Valor Amendment" to the Constitution of the United States for the purpose of providing commonsense for the Presidency.

1 *Resolved by the Senate and House of Representatives*
2 *of the United States of America in Congress assembled (two-*
3 *thirds of each House concurring therein),* That the follow-
4 ing article is proposed as an amendment to the Constitution
5 of the United States, which shall be valid to all intents and
6 purposes as part of the Constitution when ratified by the
7 legislatures of three-fourths of the several States within
8 seven years of the date of its submission by the Congress:

I

Source: House of Representatives Joint Resolution (introduced after the second assassination attempt on President Ford)

"ARTICLE—

"SECTION 1. No person shall be President of the United States who shall not have enough sense to come in out of the rain of bullets.".

"Plus all the pinto beans he can eat."

96TH CONGRESS
2D SESSION
H. R. 7349

The Former Presidential Enough Is Enough and Taxpayers Relief Act of 1980.

IN THE HOUSE OF REPRESENTATIVES

MAY 14, 1980

Mr. JACOBS introduced the following bill; which was referred to the Committee on Government Operations

A BILL

The Former Presidential Enough Is Enough and Taxpayers Relief Act of 1980.

1 *Be it enacted by the Senate and House of Representa-*
2 *tives of the United States of America in Congress assembled,*
3 That the total annual Government expenditures for the care
4 and feeding of a former President shall not exceed ten times
5 the poverty level income for one urban family of four.

○

> *"Refer it to the Committee on Mainly Irrelevant Comments (COMIC)."*

CONGRESSIONAL RECORD—HOUSE June 11, 1979

Mr. ERLENBORN. Mr. Chairman, before we move on beyond the title of the new Department, let me again suggest to the House the confusion that would arise with two DOE's. The last amendment was not agreed to, possibly because the acronym for the Department of Public Education and Youth would be D.O.P.E.Y., or dopey. So I am proposing at this time a different change in the title of this new Department. These amendments would change the name of the Department to the Department of Public Education, DOPE. These amendments would be addressed to the concerns of the private education community, church-related schools, and so forth, that the Federal Government was moving into educational policymaking and would destroy their ability as private institutions not publicly supported to set their own educational policy. I think it should be the rule that the Federal Government leaves the private sector alone so that we can continue the diversity, the rich diversity in education that we have enjoyed in the past.

Mr. JACOBS. Mr. Chairman, will the gentleman yield?

Mr. ERLENBORN. I yield to the gentleman from Indiana.

Mr. JACOBS. Mr. Chairman, I have just been penciling this out several times, and I find that it comes out to DOPE. That is "dopey." Would that be to countenance the use of narcotics in education? Or how does it relate to narcotics? Why would the gentleman want to interject, shall we say, that into the proposed Department?

Mr. ERLENBORN. Mr. Chairman, I really had not thought of it in those terms.

Mr. JACOBS. I was afraid of that.

Mr. ERLENBORN. I was thinking more on the intelligence level rather than the use of narcotics.

Mr. JACOBS. I understand. I wonder if everybody will understand, since it is, at best, ambiguous.

Mr. ERLENBORN. With the evidence of what is going on in some of our schools, it might have a dual application.

Mr. JACOBS. So that this would amount to an official recognition rather like recognizing the Government of mainland China; the new Department would recognize the use of narcotics in education?

Mr. ERLENBORN. As I understand it, the next Attorney General recently has said that he is in favor of legalizing marihuana. It likely will be the policy of this administration to legalize the use of marihuana, and since marihuana is already used extensively in our public school system, I think that the application of this acronym will have a dual application both to the intelligence level of those who propose the Department and also the practices in the schools.

Mr. JACOBS. So the gentleman is proposing that the Congress recognize the use of narcotics in education?

Mr. ERLENBORN. To not recognize it is to have one's eyes closed.

Mr. JACOBS. So the gentleman urges the adoption of the amendments on that basis?

Mr. ERLENBORN. I urge the adoption of my amendments.

Mr. HORTON. Mr. Chairman, I rise in opposition to the amendments which are basically the same as the previous amendments. I urge their defeat, because they are frivolous and of no substantive value. The Department of Education is a good title for this Department. I urge the defeat of these amendments.

Mr. BROOKS. Mr. Chairman, I move to strike the requisite number of words, and I oppose the amendments for the same basic reason and ask for a "no" vote.

Source: *Congressional Record*, June 11, 1979

"Next month, a special for the ladies!"

NINETY-FIFTH CONGRESS

ED JONES, TENN., CHAIRMAN
JOHN H. DENT, PA.   WILLIAM L. DICKINSON, ALA.
MENDEL J. DAVIS, S.C.
JIM ABERNATHY, CLERK
225-4568

COMMITTEE ON HOUSE ADMINISTRATION
FRANK THOMPSON, JR., CHAIRMAN

Congress of the United States
House of Representatives
COMMITTEE ON HOUSE ADMINISTRATION
SUBCOMMITTEE ON SERVICES
105 CANNON HOUSE OFFICE BUILDING
Washington, D.C. 20515

September 1, 1978

Dear House Employee:

    I am happy to report the success of the first month of "specials" offered by the House Beauty Shoppe. The Subcommittee on Services maintains oversight of this operation and in conjunction with the management of the Shoppe will offer another month of price reductions in September.

    September will bring the fall season and the House Beauty Shoppe will present DISCO DAZE. Every Tuesday and Wednesday, special prices will be in effect for service on hairstyles, hair coloring, and permanents. Free nail decals will be given with each manicure or pedicure at the regular price. Full details on all the specials are available by calling 225-4008.

    Hours of operation are from 7:00 a.m. to 4:30 p.m., Monday through Saturday. Service is provided for Members of Congress, staff, and the general public. The House Beauty Shoppe is located in the Cannon Building, room 139, just off the main rotunda.

    I hope you will be able to take advantage of the excellent service, outstanding expertise, and the September "DISCO DAZE" specials.

    With kindest regards and best wishes, I am

                         Sincerely,

                         Ed

                         Ed Jones
                         Chairman

Source: House of Representatives Circular

U.S. House of Representatives Beauty Shoppe
139 CANNON HOUSE OFFICE BUILDING
(202) 225-4008
Washington, D.C. 20515

SEPTEMBER "DISCO DAZE"

FOR THOSE DISCO NIGHTS......COME TO THE HOUSE BEAUTY SHOPPE FOR "DISCO DAZE" SPECIALS...EVERY TUESDAY AND WEDNESDAY DURING THE MONTH OF SEPTEMBER.

FOR DISCO DOLLS: TO COMPLIMENT HER HAIRSTYLE...A FREE HAIR ORNAMENT

FOR DISCO DUDES: SHAMPOO & BLOW DRY HAIRSTYLE
                    regularly $6.00   NOW $4.00

DISCO COLOR HIGHLIGHTS:
        SUN FLICKS   regularly $20.50 NOW $15.00
        HENNA   regularly $25.00 NOW $18.50
                * Extra Charge for Long Hair

DISCO PERM: regularly $35.00   NOW $25.00

DISCO DECALS:
            WITH EACH MANICURE OR PEDICURE AT
            REGULAR PRICE....AN ATTRACTIVE NAIL DECAL FREE

Appointments are not always necessary, but for "Clock Watchers" call 225-4008 for specific appointment and choice of stylists. The HOUSE BEAUTY SHOPPE will be open every day from 7 A.M. til 4:30 P.M., <u>except LABOR DAY, September 4th, and SUNDAYS</u>.

"Would the distinguished colleague who has been paying in marked twenties kindly desist?"

Senator Dave Durenberger

News Release

353 Russell
Washington, D.C. 20510
(202) 224-3244

Suite 550 East
Butler Square Building
100 N. Sixth Street
Minneapolis, Minn. 55403
(612) 725-6111

FOR IMMEDIATE RELEASE
ISSUED FEB. 29, 1980

CONTACT TOM HORNER
(202) 224-3244

CANDY DISH SURPLUS IS SWEET NEWS FOR GBS BENEFIT

(Washington)--Senator Dave Durenberger (R-Minn.) has some good news and some bad news in a letter he is sending to his Senate colleagues this week. The good news is that at least one fund initiated in the Senate is running a budget surplus. The bad news is that the good news is about to end.

The surprising news is that Durenberger doesn't expect any complaints about the good news-bad news letter.

Last year, Durenberger was made the keeper of the Senate candy dish, a tradition begun by former California Senator George Murphy. As part of his duties, Durenberger keeps the dish on his desk in the Senate Chambers and makes sure it is stocked with sweets. His colleagues contribute whatever they feel is appropriate to the candy fund.

In his letter to the other 99 senators, Durenberger reported that the candy dish has a surplus of almost $40. Then came the bad news. Not only is Durenberger planning to spend the surplus, he asked his colleagues to increase their contributions during the week of March 3.

Durenberger is co-chairman of a benefit March 7 to raise funds for research into a cure for Guillain-Barre Syndrome. In addition to turning over the candy dish surplus to the GBS benefit, Durenberger has earmarked his colleagues' increased contributions during the week of March 3 for GBS.

Source: Senate Press Release

"Above all, O Lord, help us to abbreviate our multitudinous polysyllabifications."

House of Representatives

THURSDAY, OCTOBER 20, 1977

The House met at 10 o'clock a.m.

Father Frank J. Sanfelippo, national chaplain of Catholic War Veterans, Milwaukee, Wis., offered the following prayer:

O Heavenly Father, as we assemble today in this arena of articulation and achievement, we lift our hearts to You!

As Divine Auditor You calculate well our every endeavor as architects of a better America.

Spare us from becoming intoxicated with the excessive exuberance of our own inexhaustible verbosity!

Help us, O Lord, to see ourselves as others see us, thus avoiding self-deception and hypocrisy.

Teach us that to lead means to serve! Instill in us those sound principles and staunch standards which will guide our responsible and productive actions.

May our earnest efforts and dedication bring about a new lift to the face of our Nation, and a new dignity to our people.

This we pray in the name of our Lord! Amen.

Source: *Congressional Record*

Picking Leaves from the Executive Branch

"Nurse O'Brien recommends rubber gloves and penicillin shots on Monday if contact is unavoidable."

MEMORANDUM

THE WHITE HOUSE
WASHINGTON

March 1, 1978

TO: ALL OEOB STAFF

FROM: PATRICIA BARIO, ASSOCIATE PRESS SECRETARY

On Friday, March 3, the Office of Media Liaison will be holding a briefing for 200 college editors. The editors are scheduled to arrive at 8:00 a.m. at the 17th Street entrance to OEOB, so you may wish to use another entrance when coming to work.

> "Every letter, every telephone call, every face to face conversation helps to sell CSC. Every one of our employees is a member of the public relations staff. The attitude of every individual is the attitude of CSC in the public mind. Every employee must be willing to cooperate in improving systems and to see that problems are brought to the right place or person for consideration."
>
> PERSONNEL DIVISION
> CIVIL SERVICE COMMISSION

Source: Civil Service Employee Creed; White House Memorandum

"Plot to dump giant chocolate cheesecake on U. S. market foiled at border."

Dec. 11 *Administration of Jimmy Carter, 1979*

Cheese and Chocolate Crumb Imports

Proclamation 4708. December 11, 1979

IMPORT LIMITATIONS ON CERTAIN CHEESE AND CHOCOLATE CRUMB

By the President of the United States of America

A Proclamation

Import limitations have been imposed on certain dairy products, including certain cheese and chocolate crumb, pursuant to the provisions of Section 22 of the Agricultural Adjustment Act, as amended, 7 U.S.C. 624, (Section 22). Those limitations are set forth in Part 3 of the Appendix to the Tariff Schedules of the United States (TSUS).

Sections 701 and 703 of the Trade Agreements Act of 1979, P.L. 96–39 (The Act), require that the President proclaim a) limitations on the quantity of types of cheese specified therein which may enter the United States in any calendar year after 1979 to an annual aggregate quantity of not more than 111,000 metric tons and b) increases in a specified manner, of the quantity of chocolate crumb now subject to certain import quotas which may be entered in any calendar year after 1979. Such limitations and increases are required to become effective on January 1, 1980.

It is provided in Sections 701 and 703 of the Act that such proclamation shall be considered a proclamation issued under Section 22 and which meets the requirements of such section.

The Act also approved bilateral agreements entered into during the Multilateral Trade Negotiations (MTN) by the United States and certain foreign countries with respect to the quantity of cheese and chocolate crumb subject to such limitations that may be imported from such countries. These agreements contained the provision that "the United States agrees to take all necessary measures to permit the maximum utilization of the quotas."

On the basis of the information submitted to me, I find and declare that the import limitations hereinafter proclaimed with respect to cheese and chocolate crumb are in accord with the requirements of Sections 701 and 703 of the Act and the bilateral agreements approved by such Act which were entered into by the United States and certain foreign countries with respect to the quantity of cheese and chocolate crumb subject to such limitations that may be imported from such countries.

Now, THEREFORE, I, JIMMY CARTER, President of the United States of America, acting under and by virtue of the authority vested in me as President, and in conformity with the provisions of Section 22 of the Agricultural Adjustment Act of 1933, as amended, the Tariff Classification Act of 1962, the Trade Act of 1974, the Trade Agreements Act of 1979, and the bilateral agreements relating to cheese and chocolate crumb approved by the Trade Agreements Act of 1979, do hereby proclaim that Part 3 of the Appendix to the Tariff Schedules of the United States is amended, effective January 1, 1980, as set forth in the Annex to this proclamation.

IN WITNESS WHEREOF, I have hereunto set my hand this eleventh day of December, in the year of our Lord nineteen hundred and seventy-nine, and of the Independence of the United States of America the two hundred and fourth.

JIMMY CARTER

[Filed with the Office of the Federal Register, 9:51 a.m., December 12, 1979]

NOTE: The annex to the proclamation is printed in the FEDERAL REGISTER of December 13, 1979.

"Negotiations are hung up again."

BILLING CODE
3195-01-M

79 4742

THE WHITE HOUSE
WASHINGTON

February 8, 1979

MEMORANDUM FOR THE

SPECIAL REPRESENTATIVE FOR TRADE NEGOTIATIONS

SUBJECT: Determination Under Section 202(b) of the Trade Act; Clothespins

Pursuant to section 202(b)(1) of the Trade Act of 1974 (P.L. 93-618, 88 Stat. 1978), I have determined the action I will take with respect to the report of the United States International Trade Commission (USITC), transmitted to me on December 12, 1978, concerning the results of its investigation of import injury which was established on its own motion. The investigation was initiated as an outgrowth of information collected in conjunction with Commission investigations Nos. TA-406-2, TA-406-3, and TA-406-4, conducted under section 406(a) of the Trade Act of 1974 and concerning clothespins from the People's Republic of China, the Polish People's Republic, and the Socialist Republic of Romania. All four investigations have concerned clothespins imported under items 790.05, 790.07, and 790.08 of the TSUS.

After considering all relevant aspects of the case, including those considerations set forth in section 202(c) of the Trade Act of 1974, I have decided to accept a variation of the injury relief recommendation made by the USITC. Within 15 days, I will issue a Presidential Proclamation authorizing that a three-year global import quota be established on wood and plastic clothespins (TSUS item 790.05) with a dutiable value not over $1.70 per gross in the amount of two million gross pins. The quota, administered quarterly on a pro rata basis, will be allocated as follows:

Source: White House Memorandum

Category	Yearly quota allocation
Valued not over 80 cents per gross	500,000 gross
Valued over 80 cents per gross but not over $1.35 per gross	600,000 gross
Valued over $1.35 per gross but not over $1.70 per gross	900,000 gross
Total	2,000,000 gross

During the course of each year, as it becomes apparent that the quota for any price bracket will not be filled for the year, then the remainder of the allocation may be reapportioned among the brackets whose quotas have been filled.

Relief is warranted for the following reasons:

    1. The social costs of denying relief would be very high, since producers are located in isolated regions in the Northeast where alternative employment is scarce.

    2. Assistance will not be costly and will not impose an inflationary burden on the economy. The major clothespin manufacturers have provided commitments to comply with the Administration's anti-inflation program.

    3. Major clothespin producers have given their assurances that the relief period will be used to modernize facilities, improve distributional channels and promote their product. These steps should put them in a better competitive position once relief is lifted.

    This determination is to be published in the <u>Federal Register</u>.

Jimmy Carter

Certified to be a true copy
Anne McQuiston

"Did they check his pockets for memos?"

THE WHITE HOUSE
WASHINGTON

CHECK-OUT FORM

The checklist below is provided to simplify procedures for your separation and to notify appropriate White House Offices of your departure. Signatures must be obtained for each item. It will not be possible to arrange for issuance of your final paycheck until this form has been satisfactorily completed and returned to the Personnel Office.

Name James M. Fallows   Date of Separation 11/25/78
Current Address 4640 Reservoir Road, DC 20007
Forwarding Address Same

1. The employee's parking permit has been removed and remains have been returned to my office.
   [signature]
   White House Branch, USSS
   Uniformed Division,
   EOB, Room 22 (Ext. 4420)

2. The clearance for Special Privileges has been satisfied with the Office of the Staff Secretary.
   [signature]
   Staff Secretary
   West Wing (Ext. 7052)

3. Equipment charged to the employee has been returned to the White House Communications Agency.
   [signature]
   Commanding Officer
   White House Communications Agency
   EOB, Room 597 (Ext. 4040)

4. The employee's final bill has been paid and his White House mess privilege has been cancelled.
   [signature]
   White House Staff Mess
   EOB, Room 403 (Ext. 2568)

5. The employee's Official or Diplomatic Passport obtained for official White House use has been returned to the White House Travel Office.
   [signature]
   White House Travel Office
   EOB, Room 87 (Ext. 2250)

6. The employee has satisfied the requirements for debriefing and deposit of presidential papers.
   [signature]
   White House Central Files
   EOB, Room 68 (Ext. 2240)

7. The White House Federal Credit Union has been notified of the separation, the employee's forwarding address, and firm arrangements have been made for the repayment of any outstanding loans.
   [signature]
   White House Federal Credit Union
   EOB, Room 45 (Ext. 2900)

8. The employee has satisfied the security debriefing requirements.
   [signature]
   White House Security Office
   EOB, Rm. 109 (Ext. 2345)

9. The White House Mail Room has been advised where mail may be forwarded.
   [signature]
   White House Mail Room
   EOB, Room 82 (Ext. 2591)

10. The employee's White House or EOB Pass has been surrendered to the Secret Service.
    [signature]
    Special Agent in Charge
    Technical Security Division
    United States Secret Service
    EOB, Room 23 (Ext. 2376)

11. The White House Telephone Switchboard has been advised where telephone calls may be referred.
    [signature]
    White House Telephone Service
    EOB, Room 09 (Ext. 2134)

12. Books charged to the employee have been returned.
    [signature]
    White House Reference Center
    EOB, Room 130 (Ext. 3662)

13. The employee has satisfied outstanding advances.
    [signature]
    Administrative Officer
    EOB, Room 4 (Ext. 2500)

14. The employee has satisfied all separation requirements of the Personnel Office.
    [signature]
    James R. Rogers
    EOB, Room 6 (Ext. 2260)

Return completed form to:
James R. Rogers
Personnel Officer
EOB, Room 6

Source: White House Form

"Didn't he create the Edsel and WIN buttons?"

THE WHITE HOUSE
WASHINGTON
January 22, 1979

MEMORANDUM FOR MEMBERS OF WHITE HOUSE STAFF

FROM: JERRY RAFSHOON

SUBJECT: State of the Union Address Talking Points

(It is important that the State of the Union speech be "sold properly. It provides us with a good opportunity - at midterm - to put the policies of the Administration and the President's philosophy in a larger context. It directly addresses the charge of "themelessness". We should not be defensive about its theme or the fact that it is thematic.)

--It is an important speech - a summing up and a look forward at mid term. It is Carter's speech. He has spent more time on it than any other speech since becoming President. There have been at least a half-dozen meetings and as many drafts - each returned with extensive Presidential rewriting.

--The President made clear that it was to be a serious, thematic speech providing the best context to date of his approach to the Presidency, his view of the nation's problems, his vision for the future. There are few applause lines - no boiler-plate political rhetoric. The impact of the speech will come from the ideas contained in it.

--The theme of the speech is that we must build a new foundation for America's future. Specifically, we must restore the confidence of our people by building a foundation for a balanced, stable economic growth; we must restore trust to the political process by building a new foundation for competent and compassionate government; we must maintain a stable peace in the world by building a new foundation based on cooperation and diversity. The speech is divided into three parts: the economy (confidence) government (trust) and foreign affairs (peace). In each section there is a brief review of the progress of the last two years and a look ahead to the priority of 1979 and beyond.

--The theme is quintessential Carter. It is positive. It reflects his propensity for long-range planning. It is moderate. It is hopeful but realistic. There is nothing contrived about it. There was no effort to "find" a slogan. "New foundation" emerged from the process of developing the most definitive statement to date of the President's approach to his job.

(The "new foundation" theme will certainly be ridiculed to some extent by commentators and cartoonists. It is important that we not retreat from it so that six months from now people will say, "Remember that 'new foundation' thing Carter tried? Whatever happened to that?" The theme will hold up in the long run if we stick with it.)

Source: White House Memorandum

"EYES ONLY, and masticate after reading."

CONFIDENTIAL

DZIMBO, THE ELEPHANT

Drafted...AF:AFW:LMRives

Clearance...AFW – Mr. Ferguson
AF – Mr. Williams

CONFIDENTIAL

CONFIDENTIAL

DZIMBO THE ELEPHANT

(To be raised by the President)

In a lighter vein the President might bring up the fact that Dzimbo, the elephant presented by President Youlou to President Eisenhower on behalf of the then member states of the French Community in 1959, is still in the National Zoo in Washington and in good health. His keepers report that he was at first inclined to be difficult and to misbehave but that he is now much better and learning a few tricks to entertain the public.

CONFIDENTIAL

Source: John F. Kennedy Collection

"Sorry, it won't match our mink tank covers."

JOHN RIETZ COMPANY
12307 ventura boulevard · studio city · california · telephone: 877-0243

January 28, 1963

Mr. John J. McNally, Jr.
Staff Assistant
The White House
Washington, D.C.

Dear Mr. McNally:

Thank you very kindly for your letter dated January 24, 1963.

Needless to say we are disappointed that the President could not accept an introduction to the automatic toilet appliance which eliminates the necessity of toilet tissue by gently cleansing with warm water, and drying with warm air.

Our intention was not to offer the President a gift, as such, but rather to bring to his attention the importance of this new way of life.

Those who are in possession of the automatic toilet seat claim it to be the most dynamic improvement in personal hygeine in this century.

We invision the automatic toilet seat to become as standard eventually, as indoor plumbing is today. What this will mean for the nation, is substantially decreased disease, and an overall improved people. However, history has proved that any major development of value in the pursuit of a healthier nation, requires much time and effort toward educating the public. Our feeling is that once the President discovers the value of the automatic toilet seat, he will want to participate in the program and development of personal hygeine for our country.

We hope you can understand our reason for wanting this relayed to the President.

Page two   January 28, 1963

Rest assured we do not want to infringe on any policy the President adheres to. Possibly there is some way we could equip the White House without any personal connotation.

Could this be a donation simply to the premises?

May we please hear from you further in this regard?

Again, thank you for your time and consideration.

Cordially,

JOHN RIETZ COMPANY

John J. Rietz
John Rietz

JTRval

GENERAL
GI 2-6/R

February 5, 1963

Dear Mr. Rietz:

In answer to your recent letter with further reference to the product you are offering, I am sorry to have to send you a disappointing reply but the President prefers not to take advantage of your generosity. I am confident of your understanding.

With the President's thanks and best wishes,

Sincerely,

John J. McNally, Jr.
Staff Assistant

Mr. John Rietz
John Rietz Company
12307 Ventura Boulevard
Studio City, California

gitf offer
hjs

Guarding our Nation

"Somehow I'm not comforted."

Early Tuesday morning, June 3, 1980, a technical problem in a computer at the North American Air Defense Command caused erroneous data to be transmitted. Some displays at the National Military Command Center and Strategic Air Command Headquarters indicated multiple missile launches against the United States; however, other systems available directly from the warning sensor system continued to confirm that no missiles had been launched. As a precaution and in accordance with standard procedures, certain Strategic Air Command aircraft and Command and Control aircraft were brought to a higher state of readiness. These aircraft were manned and engines started. One Command and Control aircraft in the Pacific took off. There was no change in overall US defense posture and, after an evaluation, all systems were returned to normal. The computer technical problems are now being assessed to determine corrective action.

Source: Department of Defense Press Release

3 min 12 sec

PROPOSED QUESTIONS AND ANSWERS

Q1. For how long a period did the SAC forces remain on alert as a result of this incident?

A1. As a precautionary measure, SAC alert forces and certain command and control aircraft were placed in an increased state of readiness. Assessment that there was no threat to the United States was made in a matter of just a few minutes. ~~From the time of the initial precautionary actions which were taken to a point when it were returned to normal status within approximately 20 minutes.~~ *was deemed appropriate to reduce the alert posture was approximately 3 minutes.*

Q7. Has an incident similar to this happened before?

A7. While there had not been an incident with these specific indications, there have been other false alarms which were rapidly and accurately evaluated as no threat to the United States. The warning systems are continually being looked at from both a technical and procedural viewpoint to minimize false alarms, while concurrently maintaining the highest possible state of vigilence.

68

June 9, 1980

MEMORANDUM FOR CORRESPONDENTS

The following statement was released Saturday, June 7, 1980:

Friday afternoon (June 6) the same computer which gave off false signals on June 3rd had another malfunction and gave off another false signal. The computer readout indicated an ICBM and SLBM attack but of a smaller nature than the June 3rd event. None of the indicators of actual missile attack registered any sign that ICBMs or SLBMs headed toward the United States. Within three minutes it was positively determined that there was a computer malfunction. The engines of some planes of the Strategic Air Command were turned on, since SAC responds automatically to any warning signal. But no planes of any kind were moved and none was sent into the air. The readiness posture of other strategic and tactical forces was not increased. The computer which malfunctioned on June 3rd was deliberately left on the line with special equipment applied to it in an effort to determine the cause of the malfunction. When the second malfunction occurred Friday we believe we detected the cause. The computer has been taken off the line to absolutely pinpoint the cause and to correct it.

END

"If you're out of sus scrofa, send two dozen used gym suits."

UNITED STATES GOVERNMENT

Memorandum

TO : Director, FBI (105-174254)   DATE: 10/13/70
        Attention: Counterintelligence and Special
                  Operations (Research Section)
FROM : SAC, Detroit (100-35108) (P)

SUBJECT: COUNTERINTELLIGENCE PROGRAM
IS - DISRUPTION OF NEW LEFT

        Detroit is proposing the disruption of the physical plant of the Radical Education Project (REP), 3908 Michigan Avenue, Detroit, Michigan. REP is a full time publishing outfit of the New Left through whose auspices numerous virulent revolutionary treatises reach the Left.

        In addition, the Black Panther Party (BPP) in Detroit receives BPP publications from San Francisco. Detroit has easy access to these papers after they arrive in Detroit.

        The Bureau is requested to prepare and furnish to Detroit in liquid form a solution capable of duplicating a scent of the most foul smelling feces available. In this case, it might be appropriate to duplicate the feces of the specie sus scrofa.

        A quart supply, along with a dispenser capable of squirting a narrow stream for a distance of approximately three feet would satisfy the needs of this proposed technique.

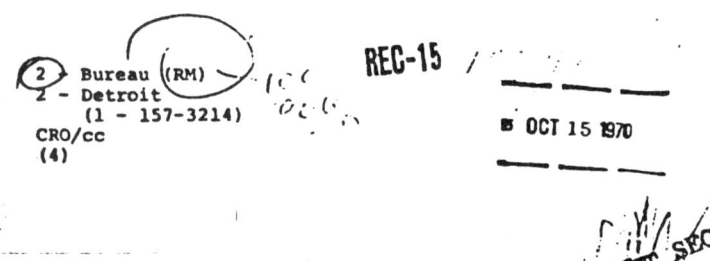

2 - Bureau (RM)
2 - Detroit
   (1 - 157-3214)
CRO/cc
(4)

REC-15

OCT 15 1970

Buy U.S. Savings Bonds Regularly on the Payroll Savings Plan

Source: Federal Bureau of Investigation Memorandum

"No ruffled parasols, please."

United States Air Force

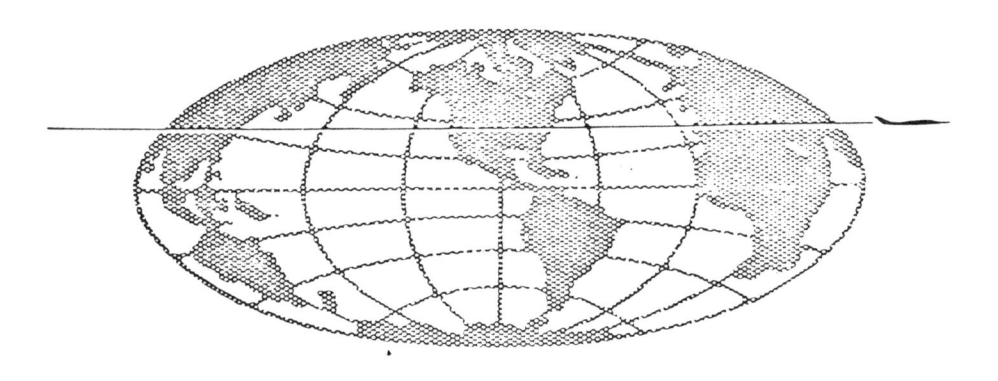

USAF UNIFORM BOARD SURVEY

USAF SCN 79-57

EXPIRES 30 APRIL 1979

FORWARD

The Air Force Uniform Board has been conducting a five-month test at the Pentaton on the Optional use of umbrellas by male personnel in uniform. Please provide answers to the following questions based on your participation in the test and the reactions of individuals you encountered while using an umbrella.

PRIVACY ACT STATEMENT

In accordance with paragraph 30, AFR 12-35, Air Force Privacy Act Program, the following information about this survey is provided:

    a. Authority. 10 U.S.C., 8012, Secretary of the Air Force: Powers and Duties, Delegation by.

    b. Principal Purpose. Survey conducted to assess opinions of Air Force members concerning the use of the umbrella while in uniform.

    c. Routine Use. Survey data will be used to evaluate guidelines for authorized use of the umbrella.

    d. Participation in this survey is entirely voluntary.

    e. No adverse action of any kind may be taken against any individual who elects not to participate in this survey.

INSTRUCTIONS FOR COMPLETING SURVEY

1. Record answers to questions on separate answer sheet. If you do not find the exact answer that reflects your opinion, use the one that is closest to it. Some questions ask for additional comments. In these cases, record your comments in the survey booklet.

2. The answer sheet is designed for machine scanning of your responses. Please use a Number 2 pencil and observe the following:

- Make heavy black marks that fill the spaces.
- Erase cleanly any answer you wish to change.
- Make no stray markings of any kind on the answer sheet.
- Do not staple, tear or fold the answer sheet.

1. What is your current active duty grade?

   A. General Officer
   B. Colonel
   C. Lieutenant Colonel
   D. Major
   E. Captain
   F. First Lieutenant
   G. Second Lieutenant
   H. Warrant Officer
   I. Chief Master Sergeant
   J. Senior Master Sergeant
   K. Master Sergeant
   L. Technical Sergeant
   M. Staff Sergeant
   N. Sergeant
   O. Senior Airman
   P. Airman First Class
   Q. Airman
   R. Airman Basic

2. During the test, how often did you use an umbrella in inclement weather?

   A. About all the time
   B. More than 50% of the time
   C. About 50% of the time
   D. Less than 50% of the time
   E. Rarely
   F. Not at all

3. What was the typical protection you used during the test in inclement weather?

   A. Raincoat only
   B. Umbrella only
   C. Raincoat and umbrella
   D. Other (Explain)

   _____

4. What comments did you receive from personnel from other services concerning use of the umbrella?

   A. Predominantly favorable
   B. Neutral
   C. Predominantly unfavorable
   D. I received too few comments to offer a valid opinion
   E. I received no comments
   F. I did not use an umbrella

5. What was the civilian reaction to your use of an umbrella while in uniform?

    A. Predominantly favorable
    B. Neutral
    C. Predominantly unfavorable
    D. I received too few comments to offer a valid opinion
    E. I received no comments
    F. I did not use an umbrella

6. What kind of umbrella did you use during the test?

    A. Small size/collapsible
    B. Standard type (noncollapsible)
    C. Oversized
    D. I used more than one type of umbrella
    E. I did not use an umbrella during the test

In the following series of questions, please circle the appropriate letter which corresponds most closely to your opinion regarding the use of umbrellas by male personnel.

	Strongly Agree	Agree	Neither Agree Nor Disagree	Disagree	Strongly Disagree	No Opinion
7. Umbrellas should be authorized as an optional uniform item for male personnel	A	B	C	D	E	F
8. It is not masculine for a male in uniform to use an umbrella	A	B	C	D	E	F
9. Use of the umbrella interferred with saluting and other military courtesies	A	B	C	D	E	F
10. I feel less military when using an umbrella	A	B	C	D	E	F

		Strongly Agree	Agree	Neither Agree Nor Disagree	Disagree	Strongly Disagree	No Opinion
11.	Use of umbrellas by male personnel reduces their professional image	A	B	C	D	E	F
12.	I experienced no derogatory remarks concerning the use of the umbrella while in military uniform	A	B	C	D	E	F
13.	Female Air Force personnel reacted favorably to my use of the umbrella	A	B	C	D	E	F
14.	Use of umbrellas detracted from the combat ready image that US military forces should project	A	B	C	D	E	F

15. If the Uniform Board authorized use of an umbrella on a regular basis, what kind of umbrella would you recommend?

    A. Small/collapsible type
    B. Standard type (noncollapsible)
    C. Oversized
    D. N/A. Do not recommend use of the umbrella

16. To what degree do you approve or disapprove of the use of an umbrella by male personnel while in uniform?

    A. Strongly approve
    B. Moderately approve
    C. Slightly approve
    D. I could go either way
    E. Slightly disapprove
    F. Moderately disapprove
    G. Strongly disapprove

    If you disapprove, please explain: _____

17. If optional use of the umbrella was adopted, would you use an umbrella at least occasionally during inclement weather?

    A. Yes
    B. No
    C. Not sure/undecided

18. If you would not use an umbrella, would you object to others using one while in uniform?

    A. N/A. I would use an umbrella
    B. Yes
    C. No

19. Do you use an umbrella during inclement weather when dressed in civilian clothes?

    A. Yes
    B. No

20. Do you have any specific recommendations regarding the umbrella itself (design, style, etc.)? If so, please note them below.

21. Have you identified any specific problems associated with male personnel use of an umbrella? If so, please note them below.